CONDOMINIUMS

CONDOMINIUMS

The Effects of Conversion on a Community

JOHN R. DINKELSPIEL

JOEL UCHENICK

HERBERT L. SELESNICK

Harbridge House, Incorporated

Auburn House Publishing Company
Boston, Massachusetts

Library of Congress Cataloging in Publication Data
Dinkelspiel, John R.   1935–
  Condominiums, the effects of conversion on a community.

  Includes index.
    1. Condominium (Housing)—Massachusetts—Brook-
line—Conversion.   I. Uchenick, Joel, joint author.
II. Selesnick, Herbert L., joint author.
III. Harbridge House, Inc.   IV. Title.
HD7287.66.D56   307.7'6'097447   80-39894
ISBN 0-86569-059-6

PREFACE

Beginning in early 1977, after the real estate market had recovered from the 1974–76 recession and when the rental market was tightening, the town of Brookline, Massachusetts, began experiencing a boom in condominium conversion. Although there had been a spurt of conversions in the early 1970's, the effects of conversions on the housing market in this in-town suburb of Boston passed largely unnoticed until mid-1977.

Brookline has a history of public concern about its housing market. In 1969 the town adopted a rent control ordinance and since that time has effectively governed the rate at which rents have increased. About 13,000 apartment units were covered by this regulation, virtually all of the nonsubsidized and nonpublicly financed multi-unit buildings in the town, comprising over half of all housing units. In addition, the town has encouraged the construction of a good deal of subsidized housing for elderly and low income persons in recent years and has on several occasions prepared studies of the housing market.

When the conversion process began to remove units from the rental stock at an increasing pace in 1977, therefore, there was an immediate reaction. The basis for the 1969 rent control ordinance had been the declaration of a "housing emergency" that the town determined was, among other things, squeezing low and moderate income households out of the market. Condominium conversion thus threatened to undermine the town's long-standing policy of preserving moderate income rental housing opportunities.

Brookline's town meeting form of government provides numerous opportunities for the rapid and direct expression of public concern about issues and problems. The five-member Board of Selectmen (essentially the town's executive body), the Advisory (finance) Committee of the Town Meeting, a housing subcommittee of the Advisory

Committee, the 240-member Town Meeting as the town's basic legis-
lative body, and tenant and property owner groups quickly became
enmeshed in a lively debate about what, if anything, to do about the
conversion phenomenon.

Brookline is a fairly small and close-knit community, and its residents have a history of active, articulate, and informed involvement in
public issues. As the debate over condominiums heated up, it became
increasingly evident that there was a great deal of contradictory—and
probably misleading—information about conversion being cited by all
sides. Tenant groups dramatized instances of eviction of long-time elderly residents by profit-seeking developers in tones that on occasion
sounded like the rhetoric of class warfare. Landlords often obliged by
playing the capitalist role to the hilt, defending their right to a fair
profit—which, they claimed, the rent control system had long denied
them.

It became evident during 1978, as the pace of conversion quick-
ened, that the debate over how, or whether, to control the conversion
process had little chance of resolution until more was known about
exactly what was taking place in the town with regard to conversion.
Ultimately the Selectmen appointed a Condominium Study Committee, which during 1978 and early 1979 formulated an elaborately detailed agenda of questions of fact as the basis for understanding the
issues requiring resolution. At the same time, the Advisory Committee
formulated its own list of issues, fairly brief but more policy oriented,
which it felt needed to be addressed.

As the debate progressed and, inevitably, became involved in the
internal power struggles of the town's governance structure, the
Selectmen's Condominium Study Committee decided that the task it
had set for itself was too difficult for a part-time group to address adequately. The Committee's goal was not simply to develop a substantial
body of detailed data but to do so in such a way that the data would
stand above the fray and not itself become the subject of the debate. It
was decided that the Committee's parent, the Selectmen, should request funds from the Town Meeting to have the questions raised by
the Study Committee and the Advisory Committee researched and
answered by professional consultants. Funds for this purpose were approved in May 1979, and Harbridge House, Inc., was selected to carry
out the study. Harbridge House, an international management con-
sulting organization based in Boston and founded in 1950, had exe-

cuted numerous community studies, including a detailed appraisal of
the operations of rent control in Brookline and in three other communities in and around Boston.

The ground rules for the requested study were explicit and restric-
tive. The consultant was to assemble factual information to answer all
of the over one hundred detailed questions raised by the two commit-
tees. The consultant, however, was not to address any policy issues;
there were to be no recommendations issuing from the report, no analyses of policy options available to the town—nothing, indeed, except
exposition and explanation of factual information that described fully
what condominium conversion was all about in Brookline and how it
was affecting the town. The study was carried out between May and
November 1979 and is presented here in a somewhat modified and
expanded form. The basic character of the study—that is, the empha-
sis on fact finding rather than on policy analysis or development—has
not been changed.

Acknowledgements

A great many officials and residents of the town of Brookline provided
support important to the successful completion of the study. Ken
Nelson, Chairman of the Condominium Study Committee, was largely
responsible for the formulation of the detailed study agenda and provided support throughout the study. Other town officials provided assistance in various ways, including Richard Leary, Executive Secre-
tary of the Board of Selectmen, and Margaret Mahoney, his assistant;
John Woodward of the Planning Department; Roger Lipson of the
Rent Control Board; and Massachusetts Representative John Businger.
A detailed analysis of Rent Control Board data files was prepared on a
computer by William Mitchell with the support of Christopher Cas-
sidy, head of Information Services. Frank Ryan, the Town Assessor,
gave hours of his time and much wisdom in analyzing assessment records.

Many developers, bankers, landlords, and others associated with the
Brookline housing market provided information and suggestions in extensive interviews. Over twelve hundred town residents cooperated
by answering an in-depth telephone interview. The telephone survey
was conducted by Becker Research, Inc., of Boston under the direction of Becker Vice President Jack Reynolds.

The Harbridge House contributors to the original study, in addition to the named authors, included John Prior, who showed remarkable ingenuity, persistence, and acumen in gathering a wide range of data and analyzing their significance. Henry Norwood and David Jones also made professional contributions, and clerical support was provided by Alake Johnson, Karen Bender, and Cynthia Iudica.

The town of Brookline, although it accepted the report and has made continuing use of its findings, bears no responsibility for the data or for interpretations of them; both data and interpretations are solely the responsibility of the authors.

THE AUTHORS

CONTENTS

LIST OF TABLES

Chapter 1

STUDY CONTEXT AND METHODOLOGY

The economy in suburban America often resembles the weather. It is usually fairly predictable, falling into a range between nice and unpleasant. But at irregular intervals the weather breaks out into blizzards, droughts, or heat waves that cause great disruptions and even catastrophes. Such events are unpredictable but powerful, and it is difficult to cope with them or to prevent the short- or long-term damage they cause. The economy, too, has the capacity to erupt unpredictably. A major plant closing causes disastrous unemployment; a new highway brings explosive subdivision development; a major new industry moves in, bringing economic good times. For some towns and big city neighborhoods, large-scale condominium conversion seems to have been added to this list of disruptive phenomena in the last decade. In one such town, Brookline, Massachusetts, it appeared for a while in the late 1970's that many of the town's rental apartments, occupied by well over one third of its population, might soon be converted to condominiums.

Concerned with the potential effects of conversion and perplexed by its sources, the town of Brookline determined to understand its causes and consequences before acting; unlike the weather, conversion could be influenced if somebody did something about it. The following pages not only describe the situation in Brookline but also present an approach to understanding the conversion phenomenon which can be applied in any community. Understanding who buys condominiums

1

and why, who develops them and why, and how a community's population and budget may be affected will help any community come to grips with the difficult social and economic policy issues that large-scale conversion raises.

Brookline in Its Local Setting

Brookline, Massachusetts, is a modest size residential community of about 58,000 people. Almost wholly bounded by the city of Boston, it has the general character of a prosperous inner suburb. The town is comprised of high-density apartment-dominated neighborhoods, areas of older single family homes on modest lots, high-priced, very elegant sections, and open spaces taken up by golf courses, parks, and even a working farm or two. Long-settled families and their children and grandchildren occupy many parts of the town. At the same time, the many moderately priced—in comparison to other nearby locations—apartments attract a large transient group of students, and many single professionals.

The people of Brookline are predominately middle income and in professional and managerial occupations. Civic spirit is strong, visible, and a major force in shaping the town's growth. Although the heart of downtown Boston is only a ten-minute drive through busy streets from the town's commercial center, Brookline has and cultivates the bearing of a distinct and unrelated community. The housing market in housing-short Boston, however, does not respect political boundaries. Students from the two dozen colleges and universities in the area frequently move in and out of Boston, Cambridge, Brookline, and adjacent neighborhoods. Real estate taxes, among the highest in the nation in Boston, are little lower in Brookline. A central location and good public transit make Brookline more convenient to reach than many parts of Boston. Brookline is, in short, an integral if distinguishable segment of the Boston housing market.

The Brookline housing stock, according to 1978 town data, was as follows. There were about 24,400 dwelling units, about 96–97 percent of them occupied. About 4,500, or 18 percent, were single family homes. The average price of a single family house on the market in Brookline in 1979 was $104,000. There were, in addition, about 5,200 two- and three-unit houses. The town established that there were about 17,500 rental units of all types, of which 9,700, or 55 percent, were rent controlled at the end of 1978. Publicly subsidized units for low income and elderly persons accounted for about 3,000 units, and another 2,600 units were FHA or similarly publicly financed noncontrolled units. Finally, by the end of 1979 close to 2,000 units had been converted from rent controlled units to condominiums since the beginning of conversion in 1970. There were also a few hundred condominiums in new nonconverted buildings.

The 1969 rent control ordinance adopted by the town fixed the rent of all units except those in two- and three-unit houses, rooming houses, and publicly subsidized or financed apartment buildings. The ordinance covered about 13,000 units in 1969, and it is in this stock that almost all conversions have taken place. Apartments constructed since 1969 are not rent controlled, but very few have been built. As of July 1979, the median rent in rent controlled units was around $300 (see Chapter 6 and Appendix C for details), and the average selling price of condominiums was around $40,000.

Brookline condominiums, in the context of the Boston area housing market, are generally moderately priced. Their average selling price in 1979, as noted above, was about 40 percent of that of single family homes on the market in Brookline. The typical unit converted, as discussed in greater detail in Chapter 6, had rented for only a little more than the typical two- or three-bedroom rent controlled apartment, which rented for $300.

Conversion activity in the Boston area has been concentrated in a few neighborhoods in Boston, Brookline, and Cambridge, which is just across the Charles River from Boston and Brookline. Conversions in Boston, in contrast to those in Brookline and Cambridge, tend to be considerably more expensive. This is only in part because of higher land values or generally higher housing prices. It is more directly a result of the far larger investment in rehabilitation which is typically made in Boston condominiums. Condominium conversion in Boston tends to involve a substantial investment by the developer in upgrading the unit, with a consequent significant change in the income level of occupants. In Brookline, by contrast, the developer's investment tends to be significantly smaller, and the change in income level of condominium owners correspondingly less significant.

The significance of the different approaches to condominium conversion found in Brookline can be better appreciated when they are placed in the context of the broad range of conversion activity nationwide.

Brookline in Its National Setting

Several broad types of condominium conversions can be identified. One, typified by conversions in Brookline, results in relatively little change in the social economic makeup of a neighborhood. The conversion process does not culminate in major physical changes in a building, and units tend to be sold primarily to people living in the community and those of similar socioeconomic backgrounds. A second type of conversion, common in Boston and elsewhere, results in a substantial physical upgrading of a building, a concomitant jump in its price class, and consequently, a significant change in the income levels and occupations of the residents. A third type, of which the Chicago Lakeshore area is the leading example, is represented by the sale of condominiums mainly to investors—that is, units are purchased and subsequently rented by the owners. This process has the general effect of raising rents significantly. Newly built condominiums—as opposed to converted rentals—whether for vacation use (as in Florida) or for year-round occupancy in suburban areas, because of their location, generally occupy a different segment of the housing market than converted units.

A recent nationwide study of condominium conversion by the U.S. Department of Housing and Urban Development (HUD) documented the location and character of most conversion activity in the nation and described the types of conversion processes undertaken.[1] The HUD study identified conversion activity in the 37 largest SMSA's (Standard Metropolitan Statistical Areas) in the country. Twelve of the SMSA's in the HUD study were categorized as having a "high" level of conversion activity. In these twelve SMSA's, an average of 2.71 percent of the rental stock had been converted; in the remaining 25 SMSA's, the conversion rate was estimated to be 1.30 percent; and in the balance of the country, 0.57 percent.[2] The twelve high-activity SMSA's accounted for 56.9 percent of all conversions nationwide be-

---

[1] U.S. Department of Housing and Urban Development, Division of Policy Studies, *The Conversion of Rental Housing to Condominiums and Cooperatives: A National Study of Scope, Causes and Impacts* (Washington, D.C., 1980).
[2] *Ibid.*, p. IV-7.

tween 1977 and 1979. In four of these SMSA's—Chicago, Denver, Houston and Washington—the rate of conversion in this period was between 5 and 8 percent of the total rental stock.

The conversion rate for the Boston SMSA, including Brookline, was calculated at 2.37 percent. For Brookline, by contrast, the rate for this period was 12–13 percent when calculated in relation to all rent controlled units and 7–8 percent when calculated in relation to the entire rental stock. The rates of conversion for SMSA's are, of course, average for an entire metropolitan area and include rates for neighborhoods in which there is no conversion activity as well as for those in which there is high activity. Nonetheless, the rate in Brookline (which also has a diversity of neighborhoods), whether taken as 7–8 percent or 12–13 percent, was high. Brookline is indeed one of the conversion hot spots in the nation, and its experience is thus both distinctive and illustrative.

The HUD study found that "conversions are not concentrated in areas with distressed rental markets but, rather, in areas characterized by tightening rental markets and strong ownership demand." [3] That is to say, high conversion activity generally reflected strength in the housing market and a tight supply-demand relationship. This has, indeed, been the case in Brookline, where rent control was imposed in 1969 because of a "housing emergency" characterized by vacancies in the 2–3 percent range. There is no indication that the housing market has significantly loosened in Brookline in the subsequent decade.

The HUD study also identified the demand for converted condominiums as coming from "a segment of the population that is not in the single family market." For these households, "converted units are not substitutes for single family homes." [4] It is evident from comparing the income data gathered from Brookline residents (see Chapter 5) with the price of single family houses on the market in Brookline (on average, $104,000) that this generalization describes the situation in Brookline well.

The pattern of conversion nationwide is characterized in the HUD study as occurring in three broad types of neighborhoods: nonresidential inner city neighborhoods, revitalizing inner city neighborhoods, and nonrevitalizing suburban neighborhoods. The differences

---

[3] *Ibid.*, p. V-11.
[4] *Ibid.*, p. V-8.

among these types relate to their location in the SMSA and to the amount of physical improvement made to a building when it is converted. Changes in the socioeconomic characteristics of neighborhood residents are most likely to take place in revitalized neighborhoods, although the HUD study generally found relatively little change in income, occupation, or racial mixture in any of the neighborhoods subject to heavy conversion activity.[5] Brookline clearly falls into the suburban nonrevitalizing category.

It should be noted, finally, that the presence of rent control in a community was not identified by the HUD study as being likely to have a significant relationship to the level or type of conversion activity. The prospect of increased owners' return on investment from converting was largely independent of the existence of rent control, as demonstrated by high levels of conversion in areas with no rent control.[6] None of the evidence collected in Brookline contradicted this finding (see Chapter 3), even though there was a common perception to the contrary among landlords.

In summary, there is good reason to believe that the characteristics of the condominium conversion phenomenon in Brookline are representative of what has happened in other active condominium markets nationwide in the past three or four years. The high level of conversion activity in Brookline serves mainly to intensify the factors associated with conversion and thus presents a richer source of data than would otherwise be available.

Study Methodology

The HUD study, which in its scope and depth of analysis is a landmark in this field, clearly depicts the forces that created the condominium movement nationwide. No nationwide study, however, can accurately predict the communities into which conversion activity will move or exactly how the local housing market or the community will react. Local housing markets and the characteristics of communities are too varied to allow such predictive certainty. What steps are necessary to build an understanding of the conversion phenomenon in a particular

---

[5] *Ibid.*, pp. VIII-31, VIII-32.
[6] *Ibid.*, pp. V-15–V-30.

community? The methodology followed in this study should provide a useful model.

Constructing such an understanding starts, analytically, with establishing which buildings are being converted. In Brookline, the Town Assessor keeps detailed records of conversions, based on his receipt of copies of master deeds, the documents that record the change in status of a building from one in which units are rented by the landlord to one in which they are individually owned. Information collected for this study from these records included the recorded transaction price, the square footage of each unit, the date of conversion, and the parties involved in the sale—all data of critical importance to understanding the situation in Brookline.

The next step requires determining which types of people are involved in the conversion—that is, who is purchasing units and who is moving out. Our study developed these data through extensive telephone interviews. A random sample of 293 condominium owners was interviewed, and a detailed questionnaire was used (see Appendix A). To obtain a sound basis for comparison, 891 renters were also interviewed, about 10 percent of whom were renting units in already converted buildings. In addition, 22 individuals whose households had been displaced by conversion were interviewed. The sample size, representing about 1,200 units out of a total of about 13,000 rent controlled or converted units, assured a high degree of reliability in the analysis of the detailed characteristics of the town's population.

One basic issue the questionnaire aimed at illuminating was how conversion was changing the town's population. Detailed questions about income, household size and composition, age, occupation, and place of prior residence provided critical information. For instance, as conversion took place, was the town's population getting younger or older? Were there more or fewer children? More or fewer married couples? Were new people moving into town or was there a lot of moving around among town residents? Comparisons among renter and condominium owner groups were essential to answering these and similar questions.

Tracking down former residents, those displaced by conversion, is always a difficult process. A substantial effort produced 22 such displaced tenants, who were interviewed for the study. Their testimony was more useful for understanding how people are directly affected by conversion than for analyzing how the town's population was being changed by conversion. In addition, renters remaining in converted buildings and others in the sample provided further data on experiences they had had with developers converting buildings.

Understanding the conversion process also requires knowing the economic incentives of developers and how developers structure their risks and opportunities to maximize their financial returns. Developers are generally dependent upon other financing sources to make possible the acquisition, remodeling, and resale of units. For this study, therefore, over twenty bankers and developers were interviewed to determine how they viewed their role. Most of these individuals were quite candid, and the information they provided, when checked against other types of data, proved generally reliable and useful. Analytic models were constructed to simulate the developer's actions and were tested against a substantial sample of data relating to acquisition costs, pre-conversion income produced by a building, value of units sold, and the like.

Finally, the study examined the impact of conversion on the town's fiscal situation—that is, on tax revenues and the demand for municipal services. Revenue impacts can be easily determined from pre- and post-conversion tax assessment records. Brookline reassesses buildings quite promptly after conversion, so these figures are representative of past assessing practices in the town. Projecting these revenue impacts into the future is more complex, and a methodology for doing this is described in Chapter 7. Changes in demand for municipal services is difficult to estimate because few empirical data are available in any town on the demand for services differentiated by type of household. Thus, it is difficult, for example, to know which local services older, more affluent households will demand more or less of in comparison to younger, less affluent households. The number of school age children in the average condominium owner's household in comparison to the number of school age children in the average renter's household was calculated from our telephone survey, and some of the possible cost consequences of the apparent change in the demand for public schools are discussed in Chapter 7.

In summary, the primary data sources for this study include a large telephone survey of renters and condominium owners, interviews with developers and bankers, and town tax and assessment records. To interpret these data, analytical models of developer behavior, future town tax revenues and costs, and potential condominium buyer behavior were constructed and are described below. These analytic and data gathering techniques owe an intellectual debt to George Sternleib and the pioneering work he did on the condominium issue. The 1976 study of the condominium conversion process in Washington, D.C., performed by Dr. Sternleib in association with the firm of Raymond, Parish and Pine was an important aid in thus study.[7]

[7] Development Economics Group, *Condominiums in the District of Columbia: The Impact of Conversions on Washington Citizens, Neighborhoods, and Housing Stock* (Washington, D.C.: Raymond, Parish and Pine, Inc., 1975).

Chapter 2

WHY PEOPLE BUY CONDOMINIUMS

Until recently, there have been two principal ways for an urban household to obtain a residence. One either rented an apartment or bought a single family house. In addition, a modest proportion of households bought two- or three-unit residences and occupied one unit and rented the others. During the 1970's a third option became available with the marketing of condominiums, single units individually owned in a multi-unit building.

The attractiveness of condominiums as a new option in the housing market can be traced to several basic demographic and housing market trends, including the growth in the number of households, due both to the diminishing size of the average household and the arrival of the baby boom generation at the household-forming age; the underproduction of new housing in relation to rising demand; and the rapid inflation in the costs of obtaining housing, which among other things made the purchase of single family houses increasingly more difficult for first-time home buyers.[1] The "invention" of condominium conversion—the transformation of a rental unit into an individually owned unit—is in effect the real estate industry's response to these trends in urban areas. Successful conversion yields significantly higher short-term returns on an investment in a multi-unit residence than renting the residence. At the same time, conversion copes with the

---

[1] See U.S. Department of Housing and Urban Development, Division of Policy Studies, *The Conversion of Rental Housing to Condominiums and Cooperatives: A National Study of Scope, Causes and Impacts* (Washington, D.C., 1980), Part 2, for a comprehensive discussion of factors associated with the popularity of condominiums.

11

shortage or absence of vacant urban land for the development of new residential units.

These statements about demographic and housing trends associated with the growth of condominiums are, however, only broad generalizations. They do not explain why an individual or a household decides to purchase a condominium in preference to other housing options. It is appropriate to begin this study, therefore, with an analysis of the motivations of condominium purchasers in Brookline. The analysis is based on the responses of 293 condominium owners to our telephone survey.

Reasons Underlying the Purchase

Condominium owners were asked to state "the one or two most important factors in your decision to buy a condominium." Approximately twenty different reasons were given but by far the most commonly mentioned was that a condominium was "a good investment." As shown in Tables 2.1 and 2.2, this reason was the one most frequently given by persons under thirty (61 percent) and by persons with less than $20,000 of annual income (48 percent). As income and age increased, investment value became less of a factor, although

Table 2.1   Condominium Owner's Reasons for Purchasing Condominium in Relation to Owner's Annual Income

	Income			Total Responses for All Households (%/No.)
Reason Cited	*Less than $20,000*	*$20,000–$39,999*	*$40,000 and over*	
Good Investment	48%	46%	45%	43% (126)
Prefer to Own	32	26	26	26 (76)
Tax Shelter	13	26	18	19 (56)
Getting Better Place to Live	13	16	19	13 (39)
Less Expensive than Renting	9	18	11	12 (35)
No Maintenance	11	16	3	12 (36)
Good Location	16	8	16	10 (30)
Already Live There	9	2	8	7 (20)
Number (N) of Households in Each Income Group	(N=72)	(N=116)	(N=38)	— (N=293)

Note: Percentages may sum to more than 100 for each group because of multiple responses.

Table 2.2 Condominium Owner's Reasons for Purchasing Condominium in Relation to Owner's Age

Reason Cited	Age						Total Responses for All Households (%/No.)
	30 & Under	31–40	41–50	51–60	61–70	71+	
Good Investment	61%	44%	40%	31%	17%	26%	43% (126)
Prefer to Own	26	30	24	25	17	21	26 (76)
Tax Shelter	16	26	20	19	8	5	19 (56)
Getting Better Place to Live	16	18	2	19	4	11	13 (39)
Less Expensive than Renting	11	12	13	11	21	5	12 (35)
No Maintenance	9	15	18	6	17	5	12 (35)
Good Location	14	9	13	8	8	5	10 (30)
Already Live There	3	3	11	6	20	16	7 (20)
Number (N) of Households in Each Age Group	(N=70)	(N=94)	(N=45)	(N=36)	(N=24)	(N=19)	– (N=293)

Note: Percentages may sum to more than 100 for each group because of multiple responses.

overall 43 percent of the sample said "good investment" was an important reason for buying. What this response pattern means, given this age/income distribution, is that condominiums are seen by households in their early years as a good way to obtain the financial security of home ownership.

That it is the financial security aspect of investment more than the income aspect which is more important for younger, less affluent households can be seen by their relatively infrequent mention of "tax shelter" as a reason for purchasing a condominium. Only 16 percent of those under 30 and 13 percent of those earning less than $20,000 mentioned "tax shelter" as an advantage, compared with 19 percent for the sample as a whole and 26 percent in the 30–40 age bracket earning $20,000–40,000 annually.

The second most frequently stated reason for purchasing a condominium was the simple desire to own a home. About 26 percent of the sample gave this as a reason, with little variance among age and income groups except for a somewhat lower rate of response among people over sixty. It seems clear, therefore, that the condominiums being sold in Brookline are seen by their purchasers as fulfilling one of the most common desires in American society—the desire to achieve the security and stability of home ownership. In Brookline, this goal was achieved among these respondents by buying a condominium that cost about $40,000. As noted later in this chapter, this amount represents about 40 percent of what it would have cost to buy a comparable condominium in the Back Bay area of Boston or a similar area or to buy an average single family home in Brookline.

Chapter 3 describes the types of buildings developers converted in Brookline and the strategies they followed. We note there that in general these developers see their primary market as people with the fairly modest, middle class, home owning goals reflected in the responses cited above. These responses take on a greater significance when one recognizes that across the country the conversion process addresses very different markets and satisfies very different needs than it does in Brookline. In the Chicago and California markets, for instance, a large portion—and in Chicago, probably a majority—of condominium units are purchased as speculative investments. They are purchased not by prospective occupants seeking to satisfy home ownership desires but by investors who have both capital appreciation (through housing price inflation) and current income (through rents) as their goals. Based on our discussions with developers and bankers, probably no more than 3–5 percent of all units in Brookline are purchased for these purposes.

It is worth noting that among the other reasons given by our sample for condominium purchase, a fairly high percentage (20 percent) of the 61–70 age group said that "already living there" was a reason for purchasing. In fact, in this age group this was the second most frequently mentioned reason, mentioned almost as often as "less expensive than renting." When the sample is divided between those who formerly rented the unit they now own and all others, 28 percent of the former renters gave "already live there" as an important reason for purchase. The former renter group gave this reason more frequently than any other reason, including "good investment," as shown in Table 2.3. The group for whom "living there already" is important is, therefore, probably much the same as the group of "comfortably retireds," identified in Chapter 6 as a significant and identifiable group of condominium purchasers. Conversion has provided the more affluent members of this older age group the opportunity to achieve greater financial security in their home occupancy.

The importance of condominium ownership to shelter a portion of one's housing costs from income taxes is also demonstrated by the responses of the sample. "Tax shelter" was the third most frequently mentioned reason for purchase (19 percent). The importance of this reason, however, did not vary consistently with either income or age,

Table 2.3   Reasons for Purchasing Condominium: Owners Purchasing Units They Previously Rented Compared with All Other Owners

| | Condominium Purchasers | | Total Responses for All Households (%/No.) |
Reason Cited	Formerly Rented Unit	All Others	
Good Investment	25%	48%	43% (126)
Prefer to Own	16	29	26 (76)
Tax Shelter	10	22	19 (56)
Getting Better Place to Live	9	15	13 (39)
Less Expensive than Renting	13	12	12 (35)
No Maintenance	9	13	12 (36)
Good Location	6	12	10 (30)
Already Live There	28	0	7 (21)
Number (N) of Each Household Type	(N=67)	(N=226)	— (N=293)

Note: Percentages may sum to more than 100 for each group because of multiple responses.

being higher for both middle age and middle income groups and lower for both higher and lower income and age groups. Thus, the overall effect of tax considerations on the ability or desire of households to buy condominiums is not easily predicted.

The primary reasons for choosing a specific unit for purchase, in contrast to the reasons for the general decision to purchase a condominium, focused on location, price, and unit/building amenities, as shown in Tables 2.4 and 2.5. Location reasons, except for work, had increasing importance as people grew older—again, a reason older renters preferred to purchase their rental units if possible. On the other hand, location in relation to work became less important as people became more affluent. In general, however, there were not great differences among age or income groups in the reasons for selecting a particular unit. This suggests, as do the data in Chapter 6, a comparative homogeneity of tastes and living styles among all Brookline condominium owners.

The importance of price in influencing the condominium-buying decision varied for different age and income groups, as can be seen in Tables 2.6 and 2.7. Less affluent people bought when they were also considering renting. This suggests that the difficulty of finding attractive, reasonably priced rental housing was a significant factor in these people's buying decisions. More affluent people appeared instead to be mainly weighing the alternatives of buying a home or buying a condominium. When the same question is looked at from the point of view of age, it is apparent that the oldest and youngest parts of the

Table 2.4   Condominium Owner's Reasons for Selecting Unit Purchased in Relation to Owner's Income

	Income			Total Responses for All Households (%/No.)
Reason Cited	Less than $20,000	$20,000–$39,999	$40,000 and over	
Unit/Building Amenities	39%	42%	42%	39% (114)
Good Location for Work	44	38	24	32 (94)
Cost of Unit	29	29	26	27 (79)
Good Neighborhood	32	21	18	27 (79)
Other Location Reasons°	34	31	21	31 (91)
Number (N) of Households in Each Income Group	(N=72)	(N=116)	(N=38)	— (N=293)

Note: Percentages may sum to more than 100 for each group because of multiple responses.
° Good location for shopping, friends, transportation.

Table 2.5 Condominium Owner's Reasons for Selecting Condominium Purchased in Relation to Owner's Age

Reason Cited	30 & Under	31–40	41–50	51–60	61–70	71+	Total Responses for All Households (%/No.)
				Age			
Unit/Building Amenities	29%	40%	33%	53%	46%	47%	39% (114)
Good Location for Work	36	39	42	31	8	—	32 (94)
Cost of Unit	24	37	31	28	8	—	27 (79)
Good Neighborhood	29	28	27	31	25	11	27 (79)
Other Location Reasons°	29	20	41	46	44	37	31 (91)
Number (N) of Households in Each Age Group	(N=70)	(N=94)	(N=45)	(N=36)	(N=24)	(N=19)	— (N=293)

Note: Percentages may sum to more than 100 for each group because of multiple responses.
° Good location for shopping, friends, transportation.

Table 2.6 Housing Alternatives Considered by Condominium Owner at Time of Unit Purchase in Relation to Owner's Income

Alternatives Considered	Less than $20,000	$20,000–$39,999	$40,000 and over	Total Households Considering Each Alternative (%/No.)
		Income		
Renting Apartment	50%	26%	32%	31% (90)
Renting House	8	4	8	6 (18)
Buying House	14	38	24	26 (77)
Buying Condominium	53	45	42	47 (139)
Number (N) of Households in Each Income Group	(N=72)	(N=116)	(N=38)	— (N=293)

Note: Percentages may sum to more than 100 for each group because of multiple responses.

Table 2.7 Housing Alternatives Considered by Condominium Owner at Time of Unit Purchase in Relation to Owner's Age

Alternatives Considered	Age						Total Households Considering Each Alternative (%/No.)
	30 & Under	31–40	41–50	51–60	61–70	71+	
Renting Apartment	36%	23%	27%	31%	38%	47%	31% (90)
Renting House	4	5	11	3	4	5	6 (18)
Buying House	24	40	20	25	4	5	26 (77)
Buying Condominium	44	41	60	50	58	37	47 (139)
Number (N) of Respondents in Each Age Group	(N=70)	(N=94)	(N=45)	(N=36)	(N=24)	(N=19)	— (N=293)

Note: Percentages may sum to more than 100 because of multiple responses.

potential condominium-buying population are more likely to be considering renting as the alternative to buying a condominium.

Overall, it appears that condominiums in Brookline are being purchased after potential buyers make a fairly broad canvass of other housing opportunities. A $40,000 Brookline condominium, after such a search, looks like "a good investment," is in a good location, sells at a good price, and is an attractive residence to buy. These are solid homebuying reasons, and thus they are likely to continue to be important factors in sustaining future demand for the type/price/location of housing represented by Brookline condominiums.

Effects of Housing Market Factors on Condominium Purchase Decision

In the minds of many potential buyers, condominiums are in competition with all other types of housing. Most Brookline condominium owners in our sample were, as noted, considering either buying a house or renting an apartment as an alternative to purchasing a condominium. Thus, the price trends of other forms of housing are directly related to condominium purchase decisions in Brookline.

While the data related to housing costs in Brookline are very fragmentary, certain general trends, shown in Figure 2.1, are clear. The most general measure of housing costs is the housing component of the Consumer Price Index (CPI), published regularly for all U.S. metropolitan areas, including the Boston area. This series shows an increase of 104 percent from the 1970 annual average through May 1979 in current dollars. While a comparable index for Brookline might show different values, the CPI does suggest the magnitude of what has been happening to housing costs in the broader market of which Brookline is a part.

One kind of data for Brookline is comparable to the CPI data on the average prices paid for single family homes in different years. Year-to-year comparisons of these data, of course, cannot reflect differences in size, quality, or other factors that may vary among the houses sold from one year to the next. Nevertheless, the figures are clearly indicative of what homebuyers in the market paid on average for a house in any given year. In 1970, Brookline homebuyers paid $56,000 and in 1979 $104,000, an increase of 86 percent—not too far from the CPI figure. Plotted in Figure 2.1 are the general rent increases allowed by

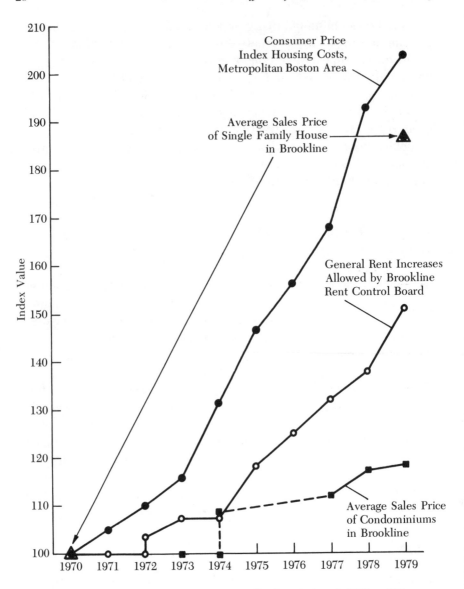

Figure 2.1　Selected Housing Cost Data. All values indexed: 1970 = 100.

the Brookline Rent Board for the majority of units since the inception of rent control. These figures show an increase of more than 50 percent over the 1970–1979 period.

In contrast to these rates of increase are the figures for the average price of condominiums sold each year in Brookline. These figures show an increase of only about 20 percent over the 1970–1979 period. There are reasons, however, that these figures are probably not representative of what has actually been happening to prices in the condominium market. First, the number of units sold annually before 1977 was so low as to make earlier data statistically unreliable. Second, it may well be that the quality of units sold over this period has not been randomly distributed. For instance, several developers have pointed out that higher-priced, better quality units are more attractive candidates for conversion. (See Chapter 3 for an explanation of developers' strategies.) This suggests that the quality of units may have been declining on average during this period as the supply of more attractive units was depleted.

A better, though less complete, gauge of the impact of inflation on condominium prices can be seen in what happens when a particular unit is resold after its initial purchase as a condominium. Based on price data for 53 units resold since 1971, an average annual price increase of 9.6 percent a year for condominiums can be calculated. This compares with an annual rate of increase of 8.7 percent a year for single family homes. This price appreciation for condominiums applies to 1978–1979, a period during which the supply of condominiums in Brookline doubled. The ability of a condominium owner to resell his or her unit during these years at a sum significantly greater than the original price in the midst of a period of ample supply suggests quite clearly a strong and continuing demand for Brookline's condominiums.

Summary

The demand for condominiums in Brookline came from a broad age spectrum of more affluent Brookline residents and their counterparts from outside Brookline who were seeking the financial security of investing in their own home. These potential buyers considered a range of other housing options, from renting an apartment to buying a house, before purchasing a condominium. They made their purchase during a time of sharply rising housing costs, and this was undoubtedly a significant factor in their decision to purchase a condominium.

The types and prices of condominiums available in Brookline appear to be well suited to the income ranges and housing needs of a significant group of Brookline residents, and these residents have purchased about half the units sold in Brookline since 1970. The reasons cited for condominium purchase and the household characteristics of the buyers suggest strongly that the demand for condominiums in Brookline, at the quality and price at which they are currently available on the market, will continue in the future as long as mortgage money is available. Condominium ownership in Brookline is an attractive housing option for a sizeable portion of Brookline's current renters as well as for those living outside the town.

Chapter 3

THE PROCESS OF CONVERTING APARTMENT BUILDINGS INTO CONDOMINIUMS

When an apartment building is converted into a condominium, the single ownership of the building is divided into separate ownerships of each apartment, or unit. The unit owners then pay ownership costs rather than paying rent. Ownership costs include mortgage payments on the individual unit (assuming the unit is not purchased for cash), a pro rata share of the property taxes on the building (the tax on the value of each unit), and a share of the operating costs of the building's common areas (costs such as those of maintaining hallways and providing heat and water), called the condominium fee.

Basic Steps and Key Participants

The steps involved in turning a rental apartment into an owned condominium unit are in principle simple:

- *Filing of a master deed.* The building owner must change the form of ownership so that parts of the building can be sold off. This is accomplished by filing a master deed. If the building has a mortgage, the form of the mortgage must also be changed to allow for the reduction of the principal as units are sold.

23

- *Rehabilitation of the building.* Ordinarily, some capital improvements are made before individual units are sold, although this is not required.
- *Sale of units.* Buyers must be found for individual units. Each buyer must finance the purchase of his or her own unit and must also accept a commitment to contribute to the building's common costs.
- *Formation of an owners' association.* Since there is no longer a common landlord, unit owners must organize to assume the landlord's duties such as providing utilities, maintaining the building, and the like. Often owners sign a management contract, perhaps with the building's developer, to perform many of these services.

In outline, this is how an apartment building becomes a condominium. The actual process, however, is far more complex. A condominium conversion is a complex real estate transaction involving a good deal of financial risk and investment on the part of developers and their financing sources. In addition, conversion sometimes involves former building owners and always involves the individual unit purchasers or their mortgage sources. The purpose of this chapter is to explain the conversion process as it occurs in Brookline clearly and realistically. To accomplish this, the process of conversion is analyzed in relation to how a developer manages it. Thus the chapter discusses, in turn, selecting a building for conversion, financing the conversion, rehabilitating the building, and marketing the building's units. These steps are examined in terms of what the developer, his or her financing sources, and his or her potential buyers must consider. Subsequently, the risks and opportunities of the principal actors in the conversion process are examined. These actors include the developer, the developer's financing sources (commercial banks), the unit buyer's financing sources (savings banks), and the former building owner. Finally, a series of models is described, based on actual experience in Brookline, which shows in typical cases how the process works in dollars-and-cents terms.

Data for this chapter were developed from two types of sources. The first source was a sample of all buildings converted. To be included in the sample, a building had to meet the following criteria: it had to have been converted since January 1, 1977, had to have achieved at least 50 percent unit sales by August 1, 1979, and had to have been under rent control. This sample was comprised of 21 buildings, representing 579 units. The second data source was interviews

conducted with eight mortgage bankers from savings and thrift institutions that fund the bulk of the condominium mortgages in Brookline, six developers representing both large and small conversion projects that accounted for a majority of the conversion activity in
Brookline, seven commercial bankers involved in the Brookline market, and numerous landlords and other parties involved in the conversion process.

Selection of a Building for Conversion

The developer of a condominium conversion may have been the
owner of the building in question for several years or may have acquired the building from a landlord in order to convert it. If the latter
is the case, building selection is the most critical strategic decision
made by the developer. In Brookline, the cost of building acquisition
accounts, on average, for 52 percent of the gross sellout price of the
units—the total sales price of all the individual units—and is by far
the largest cost of a conversion. A developer's options in acquiring a
building are limited. Developers do not have unlimited capital, their
managerial expertise can be applied to only a small number of projects at one time, and most important, lending institutions will approve
loans only for sound projects. A building that is likely to show only
marginal profits from conversion, tie up a lot of capital, and exhaust
the developer's pool of managerial talent would be considered a poor
investment by most lending institutions. From the many buildings
available for sale, therefore, a developer must be prudent when selecting a building for conversion.

In evaluating a building as a candidate for conversion, a developer
must consider many factors. Typical questions to be answered in making this evaluation include:

- Does the building have the physical characteristics that will attract unit buyers? Important considerations are whether the
  building has a good mix of one- and two-bedroom apartments, a
  desirable unit layout, a good location, parking, sound original construction, and attractive common areas.
- At what price can the building, and thus the units, be acquired
  and developed? Costs to be considered are the costs of building
  acquisition and rehabilitation, as well as potential rent loss during
  conversion, legal fees, commissions, and interest expenses.
- Who are the most likely potential buyers of the units—that is, at

what market should the project be aimed? Many Brookline developers and many bankers believe that the current tenants of a building are not only the best but also the crucial market for a successful conversion. This means that the tradeoff between a higher or lower price and more or less rehabilitation must be structured to attract the maximum number of current building residents.

- What will be the market for condominiums in the near future? Two or three years may elapse between the time a building is acquired and the final sale of all units. A developer must anticipate any changes in buyer preferences with respect to such factors as style, size, and common areas, as well as changes in prevailing housing prices.
- What is an adequate level of financing for the project? The answer to this question is based on estimates of the acquisition costs, the rehabilitation work to be done, the potential market and thus the likely selling price of the units, and the time span of the conversion and thus the time period over which the financing must extend.

Financing the Conversion

The costs of converting a building are categorized by developers as "hard costs" and "soft costs." Hard costs consist of the original price of the building and of any physical improvements made to it. Soft costs consist of all other expenses incurred on the project, including legal fees, architectural fees, survey fees, commissions to real estate brokers, interest expense on borrowed money, commitment fees paid to savings banks and thrift institutions to secure a supply of mortgage money for unit purchasers, and rental income lost while units are unoccupied either because they are being rehabilitated or because they are not sold. The total of hard costs and soft costs is the amount of money the developer must obtain if the conversion is to proceed. The difference between the total amount required for the conversion and the equity the developer can invest—the developer's own funds—is generally made up by a loan of some sort, although in some cases a private investor or venture partner supplies additional equity. The sources of debt financing available to developers include commercial banks, savings banks and thrift institutions, and the present owner of the building. The role played by each of these possible financing sources varies.

Commercial Banks. Based on our inquiries, it appears that most of the larger Boston commercial banks consider condominium conversions to be too risky to justify participation in the conversion market, given the demand for their funds in more attractive investments. Many of the medium-size and small commercial banks around Boston, however, are actively involved in this market. Lending procedures among these banks vary considerably, but a number of practices are common. Generally, the developer submits to the bank a proposal detailing the economics of the conversion, including projected costs, timetables, and selling prices. If the bank's preliminary evaluation of the proposal is positive, an inspection of the property and the building by architects and contractors is arranged. In addition, the bank usually undertakes its own analysis of the market for condominiums. Aside from evaluating the merits of the proposed project, the bank examines developer's credentials, financial background, and reputation in the field of conversions.

Two other factors are also evaluated before the bank grants debt financing to the project. First, the developer must have access to enough liquid reserves to guarantee that unanticipated difficulties will not result in the failure of the project. This means that larger developers with many other solvent investments are far more likely to obtain loans than smaller, less well-capitalized developers. Second, the developer's profit margin must be large enough to guarantee that cost overruns, less than expected income, or both, will not result in nonrepayment of the bank's debt investment. If these two factors are positive and the bank agrees to loan the developer funds, the bank normally insists that it hold the first mortgage on the property. By this mortgage, commonly called a condominium mortgage, the bank in effect gives the developer permission to pay off the loan in increments by selling individual units.

Savings Banks and Thrift Institutions. Savings banks and thrift institutions generally do not fund developers. Based on our interviews, the few times that they have done so were during periods of "loose" money when they could obtain a competitive advantage in securing the unit purchasers' mortgages by also loaning money to the developer. With a tighter mortgage market, banks have little need to secure future mortgages this way. In fact, most banks now charge developers a commitment fee to guarantee the developers the availability of mortgages for their unit purchasers.

Present Owner of a Building. The present owner, or the seller, of the building may be an important source of funds for a developer, par-

ticularly when the developer's equity and the bank loan will not en-
tirely cover the anticipated costs of the project. It has been estimated
by one developer active in the Brookline market that approximately
25 percent of his conversion projects involve financing from the sellers
of the buildings. In these cases, the seller holds the second mortgage
on the property and the bank holds the first.

From our analysis of buildings converted since the beginning of
1977, it appears that there have been only a few instances in which
long-time landlords have converted buildings themselves rather than
selling them to developers. Because most of the financial institutions
active in the Brookline market appear unwilling to permit landlords
to remortgage their buildings if the buildings are rent controlled, landlords may find that they have only two options if they wish to recover
the capital they have invested in buildings: sell the buildings to developers or convert the buildings themselves. The latter option has been
chosen by only a few landlords, it appears, because landlords generally
lack the managerial skills or the interest to become developers themselves. One landlord who sold his building to a developer explained
that he "didn't want to convert the building because of all the legal
complications and the studies I'd have to do." When he listed his
building with a real estate agent, the only interest came from developers who wanted to purchase it for conversion; no buyers interested
in operating the building as rental property appeared. In this case, the
landlord took a mortgage amounting to 20 percent of the purchase
price from the developer.

After selecting a building and arranging financing, a developer purchases the building and files a master deed. This deed, in conjunction
with a condominium mortgage given by the bank, permits the sale of
individual units.

Rehabilitating the Building

The amount of rehabilitation done on a building during conversion is
neither mandated by law nor necessarily obvious from the condition of
the building. It is based, rather, on many factors weighed by the developer. The decision about how much to invest in rehabilitation is made
after a close examination of marketing considerations. The costs of
some types of rehabilitation—for example, roof repair—can almost always be recovered in a unit's selling price. Other forms of rehabilitation, however, might encounter market resistance, such as the installa-

tion of one thousand dollars' worth of wall-to-wall carpeting in a $17,000 unit. Developers assess the price range in which the units are likely to sell and then determine which of the many possible rehabilitation investments can be justified in terms of a likely selling price and their desired return on investment. The greater the amount invested per unit, the higher the unit price will be and, probably, the less likely the tenants in the building will be to be able to afford to purchase their units.

Most bankers carefully evaluate the relationship between the investment in rehabilitation and the retention of current tenants and insist on specified levels of presales[1] before they will advance funds to a developer. This is a sure way of testing whether the combination of the amount [and cost] of rehabilitation and the basic unit cost will attract sufficient buyers at the projected selling price. For a number of reasons, explained further below, developers usually attempt to structure a conversion to maximize presales. Thus, the decision about the extent of rehabilitation is closely related to tenant-retention considerations.

Most developers in Brookline make some cosmetic changes in the course of conversion such as painting and papering units and common areas. Beyond this, two levels of rehabilitation are usually considered: the systems in the building and the basic structure of the building. Building systems include heating, plumbing, electrical wiring, and the roof. A sound roof is a necessity for virtually any building. Other systems are usually repaired as well unless the cost of doing so is exorbitant. Such repairs represent one of the areas of risk for a developer. Major improvements to a building's plumbing system may be required, for instance, but the cost of the improvements may push the unit out of the resaleable price range. The developer may then choose to transfer this risk to the unit purchasers, in theory telling them of the defect. This, of course, may make the unit difficult to sell or may make it more difficult for the unit buyer to obtain a mortgage.

Changing the structure of a building—for instance, making two-bedroom apartments out of three-bedroom apartments—is the most extreme form of rehabilitation. Such changes cause not only tenant displacement but also a major change in the income level of potential unit occupants. Because of the high price that must be asked for the

---

[1] Presales are unit sales commitments made around the time the landlord sells the building to the developer. They need not be made only to existing tenants.

units, the income levels of unit owners after conversion will likely be significantly higher than that of the pre-conversion tenants. There is little indication that this type of rehabilitation is occurring on a significant scale in Brookline, although it is prevalent in downtown Boston.

On average, our investigations reveal that between three and ten thousand dollars per unit is invested in rehabilitation of all types.

Marketing the Units

Although the formal marketing of converted units does not occur until after building selection, acquisition, financing, and rehabilitation have taken place, marketing considerations are an important factor in each of these earlier phases. The major marketing decision to be made concerns the offering price for each unit. The developer must balance two conflicting pressures in establishing this price: speed of sales and profit margin. A developer can set a very low price for units and thereby increase the likelihood of a quick sellout. This strategy, however, decreases expected profits. Alternatively, a developer can set a very high price for units and thereby increase expected profits, but this course of action may slow the pace of sales and will tie up capital longer, raising costs and increasing the difficulty of selling all units. Between these two extremes can be found a price range that optimizes the risk/ return profile of the developer. In Brookline, this range is determined partly by the demand for condominiums and partly by the developer's rehabilitation investment and other cost decisions.

What in fact, has been the range of selling prices of converted buildings in Brookline? For a sample of 21 buildings containing 579 units, a condominium on average sold for 118 times the monthly rent charged for the unit before conversion. Although the number of times monthly rent previously charged ranged from a low of 79.47 to a high of 197.84, more than 70 percent of the units fell within the range of 100 times to 130 times monthly rent; in general, then, a developer in Brookline has this latitude in establishing the asking price for a unit. Units extensively rehabilitated, those with prices representing a multiple of monthly rent greater than 130, or those with both characteristics are likely to encounter market resistance, particularly among existing tenants. While quite a few units have been sold at multiples greater than 130, there is a greater risk for both the bank and the developer in asking a sales price higher than the 130 multiple. Thus in general developers attempt to structure a conversion so that their hard and soft costs plus their expected profit can be covered by pricing units in a range representing 100 to 130 times monthly rent previously paid.

While the sales price/rent ratio is a common way to describe the price range of condominiums, price per square foot is a more familiar measure to many people. The 579 units in our sample sold for between $17.98 and $50.25 per square foot. About 70 percent of the units, however, were priced between $27.87 and $34.26 per square foot.

Another aspect of marketing strategy is to offer discounts to existing tenants. This practice is fairly common: 60 percent of the condominium owners in our survey who were formerly tenants in the buildings they now own reported that they had received a discount on the general offering price. The discounts averaged around two thousand dollars and varied from 5 percent to 10 percent of the market price of the unit. One of the larger developers active in Brookline reported that he regularly offered tenants a 10 percent discount good for 30 to 60 days. Some developers extend the discount period beyond this; others increase the discount if the tenant is willing to forego some rehabilitation of the unit.

Often, the price of a unit is raised at least once and sometimes two or three times during the period of sale as the number of available units decreases. These price increases apply to both tenants and others. The general rationale for this is twofold. The pressure for quick sales is greatest at the beginning of the sales period because the developer wants to recover costs and pay off the bank mortgage. The developer is therefore willing to accept a lower profit margin to assure these aims. Conversely, when the buildings is closer to being sold out, the unit buyer has more assurance that the conversion will be successful; thus because risk is lower the asking price is higher. Moreover, if the sales period extends for a year or more, prices for comparable units in other buildings will probably increase and the developer will wish to take advantage of this. In general, if a developer finds many willing buyers, he may conclude that he has underpriced the units and as a result will raise prices; the reverse would occur should few buyers be discovered for the units.

Developers' marketing programs usually include one or more of the following elements in addition to price variations:

- *Financial Inducements.* Twenty percent of the condominium purchasers surveyed reported they had been offered some financial inducement beyond a price discount. These inducements fell into two categories: additional renovations and improvements; and mortgages with lower than market interest rates. Developers sometimes arrange for lower mortgage rates by paying a commitment fee to a savings bank, which in return guarantees mortgage availability and low rates.
- *Model Apartments for Potential Purchasers to Inspect.* Vacant rehabilitated, furnished units are often displayed so that potential purchasers can get a better idea of what an unrehabilitated unit they may be considering for purchase will look like.
- *Advertising in the Media and Listing with Real Estate Agents.* Although the use of advevtising and real estate agents is not uncommon, neither marketing technique is heavily relied on by developers in the Brookline market because of the current high-demand market. The availability of units is often "advertised" largely by word of mouth, and the demand thereby generated is sometimes sufficient to sell many of a developer's units.

Risks, Resources, and Returns

Each of the participants in the conversion process contributes certain resources—whether they be managerial expertise, market knowledge, or funds—takes certain risks, and hopes for certain returns on his or her investment. Understanding the incentives and motivations of conversion participants is critical to understanding why the conversion process takes place in the manner it does in Brookline. The resources, risks, and returns of developers, banks, and building owners are examined in this section.

The Developer

The developer's function in the conversion process centers on the following activities: selection and acquisition of a building for conversion; construction of a financial package to carry through the conversion; rehabilitation of the building and its units; and marketing of the units. Each of these four activities has distinct risks associated with it. The developer may attempt either to minimize these risks or transfer them to other participants in the conversion process. To the extent that the developer assumes a risk, he or she expects to receive a commensurate return.

Building Selection and Acquisition. This activity has one overwhelming risk: The building acquired by the developer may turn out to be unsuitable as a condominium and will then have to revert to an apartment building or have many vacant units. This condition can occur for reasons not associated with the building—for instance, if mortgage money dries up. Although unsuccessful conversions have heretofore not been a problem in the Brookline market, failure to convert successfully is nonetheless the central consideration for developers and their primary lenders. When failure does occur, the consequences can be financially disastrous. Both developers and lenders are aware of the huge inventory of unsold units that typified the condominium market in the early 1970's and the accompanying financial ruin of the developers of those units.

After making a careful assessment of the building in question and of the supply-demand characteristics of the condominium market, the developer is left with one basic risk-minimizing option and one basic risk-transferring option. Risk can be minimized by restricting purchases to only those buildings whose purchase price is close to its value as a rental property. Should the building not be successfully converted the developer can then rent it and thereby support the original investment. Any rehabilitation investment might not be recovered, but the major investment, the building, will not be jeopardized.

Another option available to the developer is to agree with the building's owner to purchase the building only if a minimum number of presales are made by a specific date. The building thus remains the landlord's until the specified number of presales is achieved. By this means, the developer in effect transfers some of the risk of an unsuccessful conversion to the seller of the building.

Constructing a Financial Package. In constructing a financial package—funding for purchase, rehabilitation, and soft costs—the developer addresses two risk factors.

- How much time will elapse before the units are sold? That is, how long will the borrowed funds be needed?

- Will there be sufficient mortgage money available at a reasonable interest rate for unit purchasers at the time of sale?

The first risk factor is managed through a condominium mortgage. This form of building mortgage permits the developer to sell off the building by units and concomitantly provides for the gradual repayment of the developer's mortgage as the units are sold. Generally, a portion of the condominium mortgage is repaid in a specified amount whenever a unit is sold. The interest rate the developer pays on such a mortgage varies in relation to general credit conditions, to the value of the collateral represented by the mortgaged building, and to the developer's own financial situation. One banker active in the Brookline market explained that on average a condominium mortgage is outstanding for up to three years, the usual target for selling all units. The interest rate charged on the unpaid balance increases at the end of each year, and the timing of the repayment is tied to unit sales.

Ordinarily, the bank mortgage is paid off before all units are sold, usually after 75 to 85 percent are sold. This arrangement has the effect of making most of the developer's profit dependent on the sale of the last few units. A developer anxious to capture profit may press hard to sell the remaining units, perhaps at a lower price. Alternatively, the developer may be willing to hold on to them as rental units in the belief that their price will appreciate. A small developer having few other assets and with much of his capital tied up in the conversion will probably be more anxious to sell. But large developers may also be anxious to sell out quickly if they see other opportunities to invest the remaining capital/profit more favorably.

A second risk factor, the availability and cost of unit purchasers' mortgages, can be managed by the developer by arranging guaranteed mortgage availability with a savings bank or other institution funding the unit purchasers' mortgages. The developer ordinarily pays the savings bank a commitment fee for this guarantee at about the time he or she purchases the building. In return for this fee, the savings bank guarantees the availability of mortgage money to all or—more usually—some potential unit purchasers. On occasion, not only is mortgage money availability guaranteed but also the money's cost, the interest rate on the mortgage. Because developers and bankers almost unanimously agree that the greatest threat to the condominium market is the nonavailability of mortgage credit for unit purchasers, often called "end loans," recourse to this risk-reducing mechanism can be expected to increase significantly as credit tightens.

Unit Rehabilitation. For several reasons, rehabilitation—especially if it is extensive—is often viewed by developers as the most risky aspect of their investment. First, events with major cost consequences which are beyond the control of the developer may occur—for instance, unanticipated construction problems. Aside from their direct expense, these problems are costly because they delay the rehabilitation and therefore the sale of units. If the project is delayed, the expenses of real estate taxes (which must be paid during rehabilitation), interest on borrowed funds, overhead, and the opportunity cost of the invested equity may threaten the profitability of the project. In addition, the steady inflation in rehabilitation construction costs adds to the cost of completion.

In Brookline, developers prefer to avoid buildings requiring extensive rehabilitation. Rather, they have concentrated on buildings in which a small to medium-size investment in rehabilitation significantly increases the attractiveness and hence the value of the units. One active developer in the Brookline conversion market stated that he would not convert a building in which more than $5,000 per unit was required for rehabilitation. Improvements not made by the developer can subsequently be made by a unit purchaser or by all unit purchasers through their management association, in which case they are normally charged a lower price for the units. By such means, the risk of making improvements is passed from the developer to the unit purchasers.

It is interesting to note, by contrast, that in the Back Bay area of Boston, for instance, extensive rehabilitation of four- to eight-unit townhouses is a common practice. Such rehabilitation results, among other things, in prices two to three times higher than those in Brookline, both in terms of the sales price/rent ratio and square foot costs. Associated with this practice is a drastic change in the character of building occupants from students and middle income renters to upper income owners. Making major changes in socioeconomic groups is not the objective of most Brookline developers. Indeed, causing such socioeconomic changes in the tenant population is seen in Brookline as a high-risk development strategy and thus is almost always avoided.

Marketing and Pricing. The pricing of units presents the developer with at least three issues on which decisions must be made. The nature of these decisions determines, to a large extent, the success of the project. These decisions concern:

- Setting appropriate market prices for the units.
- Offering discounts to tenants.
- Increasing prices after initial sales.

The first two decisions are made before any units are sold. The developer evaluates where between the low price/fast sellout strategy and the high price/slow sellout strategy the most effective marketing approach will be found. The more conservative strategy will probably produce an income distribution among unit purchasers closer to that prevailing in the rental units before they were converted; a more radical strategy would destroy the existing income distribution of rental units by creating only expensive units.

What have been the primary strategies of Brookline developers? Table 3.1 displays the data from our sample of 21 buildings and 579 units. The least expensive condominiums sold on average for $35,227. Before conversion the units rented on average for $281.37 per month, and they were in buildings that on average had 15.75 units. The medium-priced units sold for $37,571, had rented for $318.53 per month, and were in buildings that had 27.14 units. The high-priced units sold for $43,023, had rented for $371 per month, and were in buildings that had 44.17 units. In all price ranges, the relation between pre-conversion rents and post-conversion prices was fairly consistent. The sales price/rent multiplier, however, was highest for the low cost units and decreased as the cost class increased. This phenom-

Table 3.1   Average Unit Data by Price Class of Condominium

Unit Price Class	Number of Units per Building	Unit Selling Price	Unit Selling Price	Pre-Conversion Rent per Month	Sales Price/ Rent Ratio per sq. ft.
High	44.17	$44.40	$43,023	$371.00	115.96
Medium	27.14	$31.25	$37,511	$318.53	117.76
Low	15.75	$26.55	$35,227	$281.37	125.20
Total†	27.6	$36.36	$39,664	$335.42	118.25

Note: Number in each cell represents the mean value for all units in the price class in question.
° Units are assigned to price class based on the following selling price per square foot: high, $35.50/ft² and over; medium, $29.50–$35.49/ft²; low, $29.49/ft² or less.
† Number of units in sample = 579; number of buildings in sample = 21; totals are weighted averages.

enon may be attributable to the larger proportionate rehabilitation investment made in the lower priced units. Thus the pricing behavior of developers operating in Brookline is closer to the low price/fast sellout strategy than to the high price/slow sellout strategy.

Representative Income Statement. Based on our survey of converted buildings, interviews with bankers, and data supplied by developers, we have constructed a representative income statement that reflects the general experience of developers in Brookline.

Income Statement (no broker's fee included)

Sales price per unit	$39,664
Costs per unit:	
Acquisition costs	$20,625
Conversion costs	$11,105
Total costs per unit	$31,730
Profit per unit before tax	$ 7,934

Another way of analyzing the same information is to ask what happens to each dollar a condominium buyer pays.

As Figure 3.1 shows, a little over half the price of a condominium represents the cost of acquiring the former rental apartment; over one quarter of the price is attributable to the process of changing the form of ownership of the unit and rehabilitating the unit; and about one

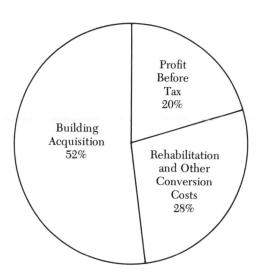

Figure 3.1 Average Distribution of Condominium Price.

fifth of the price represents the developer's gross—before tax—profit. It should be noted that these are representative figures only. Some developers claim to make a much smaller profit whereas others have demonstrated larger profits. Our analysis, which is based on data from many sources concerning various costs in the conversion process, suggests that a return averaging 20 percent of the total sellout price of a conversion is, in broadest terms, the lure that attracts developers into the Brookline conversion market.

Commercial Banks

The commercial banks that finance developers are subject to many of the same risks as developers. The risk-reducing and -transferring techniques available to these banks, however, are more numerous and potentially more effective than those available to developers. In addition, because banks assume less risk on building conversions than developers, it is not surprising that on average banks' return on investment is also less.

Bankers are very much aware that the potential success or failure of a conversion varies considerably among buildings and developers. The skills required to convert a small 6-unit building needing extensive structural changes are qualitatively quite different than those required to convert a 100-unit building in good condition but needing a strong marketing program. Bankers will, therefore, fund only those developers whose "chemistry"—to quote one banker—matches the needs of the proposed conversion. This means that experienced developers whose profit-generating ability has been demonstrated on previous conversions have a significant advantage over untried developers in acquiring debt investment from banks. By the same token, the absence of experience and credibility may be a significant barrier for prospective entrants into the conversion market.

Banks, like developers, cannot know in advance which projects will be successful. However, banks can structure their loan conditions so that funds are made available only for the most promising projects. For instance, a loan from a bank to a developer can be made contingent on the developer's securing an available supply of mortgage money (usually from another bank) for the unit purchasers. In this way, commercial banks can avoid investing in projects whose profitability may be jeopardized by a mortgage squeeeze and the consequent failure to sell all units. Another less commonly used method is for the commercial bank to make its loan contingent on presale achievement—that is, obtaining firm options to buy from a large number—perhaps 50 percent—of potential unit purchasers. In such a case, the bank finances only those projects that have already shown significant market acceptance.

After deciding which developers and which projects to fund, banks must decide how much debt to invest in projects. Here banks have several risks and returns to balance. On one hand, a bank wants the developer to have sufficient capital to complete the conversion profitably. On the other hand, the bank wants the developer to have a large enough equity investment in the project to leave sufficient capital to cover the bank's investment if a loss is incurred. Reflecting these considerations, banks active in the Brookline market have similar policies regarding the maximum they will lend to developers. This maximum varies from 75 percent to 80 percent of the building acquisition cost (note that the conversion costs may add, as illustrated in Figure 3.1, over 50 percent to the acquisition cost). The maximum, however, is not rigid. In instances in which developers have other assets to cover a loan, banks will lend beyond this limit.

After deciding how much to invest in a project, the bank must establish a repayment schedule. The bank is virtually always the first mortgagee in lending to a developer. The mortgage, therefore, is partly retired each time a unit is sold. One bank's repayment schedule requires that 85 percent of the proceeds of each unit sale be paid to the bank until the mortgage is fully retired. Thus, the bank's investment in the project ends when 70 to 75 percent of the units are sold.

Although the rates charged on conversion loans vary, a typical loan to a medium-size developer costs about 1.5–2.0 percent above the prime lending rate, plus two to three points (prepaid interest). In addition, some banks require the developer to establish and maintain a depository relationship with the bank. Even at these rates, some bankers maintain that this type of lending is no more profitable than other lending because of the risky nature of the conversion business and the high costs of servicing such loans.

In sum, the commercial bank must share many of the developer's risks. To protect itself, the bank establishes various payment conditions and higher charges. In many senses, the commercial bank and the developer are partners; hence the attitude of these banks—for instance, in relation to how willing they are to make funds available—is a key factor governing the rate of conversions in Brookline.

Savings Banks

Savings banks in Brookline and in surrounding communities generally have shown an acceptance of the condominium concept, and almost all regularly provide mortgage money to unit purchasers. The banks' lending policies, however, generally vary from the lending policies for single family homes for the following reasons: (1) The condominium concept is still new and, as one banker stated, "Bankers approach new phenomena conservatively." (2) A condominium owner is subject to more economic forces beyond his control than the owner of a single family home. A single family homeowner, for example, ideally undertakes only those repairs and improvements he or she can afford. A condominium owner, on the other hand, must be prepared to pay a share of the costs of any repairs and improvements the condominium association decides to undertake. (3) Some savings banks will fund a mortgage for a condominium only if they can be the mortgagee for 51 percent of the units in the building. If a savings bank customer wants to purchase a unit in a building in which the bank has no participation, the customer will find a more conservative response than when seeking funding for a mortgage for a single family home. (4) During times of tight money, some lending institutions will fund mortgages only if they can sell the mortgages in a second mortgage market such as the Federal Home Loan Mortgage Corporation. Some of these secondary markets, however, are not open to condominium mortgages unless the building in which the condominium is located previously has been approved for this market. Many older condominium buildings were developed when the secondary mortgage market was not a large financing factor and thus do not have the necessary approval. As a result of these four factors, a condominium purchaser generally must meet higher down payment requirements than the purchaser of a single family home and is also subject to a somewhat higher interest rate, usually in the form of added points.

Some savings banks will fund mortgages for no more than a few units in any one converted building but others, as noted, insist on holding the mortgages for a minimum of 25 or 50 percent of the units in a building or even for 100 percent of the units. Banks requiring a large participation in a building do so for two reasons. First, there is an economy of scale. For example, the costs of inspecting one building can be spread over each unit for which a mortgage is funded, thus reducing the servicing costs per mortgage. Second, by participating in the financing of at least 50 percent of the units the bank is in a position to step in and exercise control of the building if the building gets into financial difficulty. This might happen if a major repair or accident caused several owners to default on their building maintenance fees.

Savings banks, then, are generally not critical factors in the initial development of a conversion. Their role is of considerable importance, however, in the ultimate sellout of the units in a building. As long as mortgage money is fairly easy to obtain, savings banks will have little influence on the rate of conversion of buildings, but as mortgage money tightens they will become perhaps the most critical link in the conversion process. If unit purchasers cannot get mortgages, the conversion process will quickly slow down or even stop, as it did in 1975–1976.

Apartment Building Owners

Apartment building owners in Brookline are always confronting four options.

- Continue as landlords.
- Sell their buildings to other landlords.
- Convert their buildings into condominiums themselves.
- Sell their buildings to developers for the purpose of conversion.

Conversion, as has been noted, is a knowledge-intensive activity requiring skills in finance, construction, and marketing. Only a few landlords have undertaken the risky tasks involved in conversion. Nevertheless, a landlord has certain advantages over a developer in converting a building himself. Already owning the building, the landlord avoids the time and cost of the search procedure the developer must engage in to find a desirable building. Moreover, the bank holding the mortgage on the building may be a willing source of financing. If the mortgage on the building was written when interest rates were low, the bank may be quite interested in the opportunity of converting it to a condominium mortgage with a higher interest rate. On the other hand, few banks are willing to refinance a rent controlled building. To the present owner, these considerations mean that in terms of existing debt there are incentives to convert the building and disincentives to continue renting the building.

Many Brookline owners, as history shows, have decided to sell their

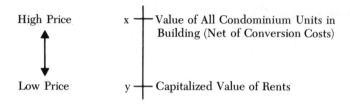

Figure 3.2   Relationship Between Building Price and Expected Profit.

buildings to condominium developers. As sellers, owners have two primary concerns: price and terms of sale. In our interviews, some developers and bankers argued that a landlord can obtain better terms and
prices by selling to a developer for conversion rather than to another
landlord. A developer, according to this argument, can afford to pay
more for a building than a prospective landlord can because the
developer's future profit potential is higher than the landlord's. The
relationship between the relevant variables is shown in Figure 3.2. In
cases in which the profit a developer wants is less than $x - y$, the
developer can afford to offer more for the building than the prospective landlord can. Our discussions with other developers, however,
suggest that even if developers intend to convert a building they will
probably offer to pay only the capitalized value of the rent. If this is
true, building owners wishing to sell might have little preference between developers and landlords.

Price is not the landlord's only consideration, however. In cases in
which a developer and a prospective landlord offer the same price for
the building, the terms may differ significantly. For example, both
types of purchasers may require the landlord to take a second mortgage as a condition of purchase. The developer's second mortgage,
however, will most likely be of much shorter duration than the prospective landlord's. The developer's second mortgage will be structured like a condominium mortgage—that is, it will be repaid as units
are sold. With an average two- to three-year sellout period for the
project, the seller's exposure would be limited to this period whereas
the landlord/purchaser would probably offer a five- to ten-year pay-
back period. But the integrity of the developer's second mortgage is
tied to the success of the conversion, arguably a high-risk undertaking.

The largest risk a landlord takes in selling to a developer, however,
is that the developer may withdraw from the conversion after signing
the purchase and sale agreement and not buy the building after all.

Moreover, if the developer begins marketing the units before the purchase date, some of the tenants may move and the landlord will have to rerent the vacated units. The seller can minimize this risk by restricting the buyer's options through a tightly drawn purchase and sale agreement of short duration.

In sum, the pros and cons of a landlord selling to a developer or to another landlord are mixed. A more basic question, however, is whether the landlord wishes to sell the building at all. We found no evidence that any substantial number of rent controlled buildings are now on the market in Brookline. It appears that most landlords in Brookline, after weighing the alternatives open to them, still prefer to continue to rent their buildings. It can be argued that this may be because their income from renting and the other satisfactions of ownership (for instance, being able to pass on a sort of "living trust" to their children) meet their needs. Or, as one developer suggested, it may be because rent control has depressed the value of rental buildings and landlords do not want to sell at prices they consider to be below the buildings' real value.

Regardless of what landlords' actual reasons are—and reasons certainly vary among landlords—it does not appear that the desire of landlords to sell their buildings is a major force in pushing up the rate of conversions. As discussed in Chapter 7, the availability of developers with the financial ability and range of skills necessary to convert buildings successfully, the assistance offered by banks, the rising demand for the form and price of home ownership represented by condominiums, and the effects of conversion regulations seem to be the most significant factors influencing the rate of conversions.

Three Models of Conversion

The foregoing discussion delineated in qualitative terms the elements of the conversion process and the risks and resources of conversion participants. Our investigations revealed that developers of different sizes and with different resources combine these elements in characteristically different ways. This section presents in quantitative terms three models for developing a condominium which different types of developers have followed in Brookline. The data for each model are drawn from information provided by a number of developers and

Table 3.2   Alternative Development Models

Model	Number of Units per Building	Selling Price per sq. ft.	Unit Selling Price	Pre-Conversion Rent per Month	Sales Price/Rent Ratio
Model A	60	$43.00	$44,500	$385	116
Model B	12	$26.00	$41,200	$295	139
Model C	15	$31.00	$34,500	$350	100
Average of Sample of 21 Buildings (for comparison only)	27.6	$36.36	$39,664	$335.42	118.25

banks in relation to specific buildings they have developed or financed. We have tested the reliability of these information sources by comparing the numbers from different sources for the same building and by our own financial analyses of typical conversion situations.

The three models we describe, therefore, are firmly founded in verified empirical data. At the same time, they do not replicate the experience of any one developer or any one conversion. Each model is representative of a different general approach to converting an apartment building to a condominium. Most of the conversions in our sample of 21 are explained by one or the other of these models. Table 3.2 summarizes the data for all three models.

Model A

Model A characterizes condominium conversion projects that require a large equity investment for building acquisition. Such conversions, which usually occur in buildings containing a large number of units (in our sample, 40 or more units), require substantial front-end equity from the developer—that is, a substantial investment of the developer's own capital. The few developers who undertake these high-cost conversions are well capitalized and have relatively easy access to loan funds.

Based on our data for this model, the typical number of units per building was 60; the typical unit selling price per square foot was $43; the typical unit selling price was $44,500; the average rent for a unit before conversion was $385 per month; and the average selling price of a unit represented 116 times the previous monthly rent of the unit. Model A has, relative to the other models, the highest selling price per square foot, the highest unit selling price, the highest pre-conversion rent per month, and a mid-range sales price/rent ratio.

The income statement on page 37 shows the typical financial considerations of a developer following Model A.

Model A

Sales price per unit	$44,485
Costs:	
Acquisition	$24,912
Conversion	$10,676
TOTAL COST	$35,588
Profit before tax (no broker's fee included)	$8,897
Gross sellout price	= 100%
Acquisition	= 56%
Conversion	= 24%
Profit	= 20%
Developer's Equity Investment	= $16,895
Return on Equity	= 21.5%°

° This percentage represents an internal rate of return on the developer's own funds, assuming no recapture of investment and profit for two years. The rate of return on equity is directly related to the proportion of the total investment in conversion that is the developer's money. Profitability is computed on the total investment base—the developer's funds and all other invested funds in the conversion, or all debt and equity. Most real estate transactions have a comparatively high return on equity because they have a narrow equity base.

Generally, Model A conversions involve the acquisition of high rent units in relatively large buildings that require little more than cosmetic rehabilitation. Developers using this strategy invariably have been the owners of a large amount of rental property. Because of their financial strength, these developers can follow a slower pace of conversion. In addition, the tenants in the building being converted are among the most affluent renters in the Brookline market. This combination of slow pace and affluent tenants is highly correlated with a large number of presales. The need for little rehabilitation and the high number of presales result in a low risk albeit expensive conversion. Selling price, as measured by the sales price/former rent ratio, is slightly below average for our sample of 21 converted buildings. Thus, on the low price/fast sellout—high price/slow sellout spectrum, the Model A strategy falls about midway between the extremes. Based on our analysis, we believe that this strategy is by far the one most frequently employed in Brookline since 1977.

Model B

Model B characterizes condominium projects that require a greater than average rehabilitation investment. Building acquisition, as a result, is not the only large cost facing the developer; rehabilitation is also a major cost. These conversions tend to be undertaken by developers who either are contractors themselves or are linked closely with contractors.

Our data show that for Model B the typical number of units per building was 12; the typical selling price per square foot was $26.00; the typical unit selling price was $41,200; the typical rent before conversion was $295 per month; and the sales price/rent ratio was 139—the highest for any model. The following income statement shows a developer's typical financial considerations in this strategy.

Model B

Sales price per unit	$41,444
Costs:	
Acquisition	$18,649
Conversion	$14,505
TOTAL COST	$33,154
Profit before tax (no broker's fee included)	$ 8,290
Gross sellout price = 100%	
Acquisition = 45%	
Conversion = 35%	
Profit = 20%	
Developer's Equity Investment = $7,771	
Return on Equity = 26.6%°	

° This percentage represents an internal rate of return to the developer's own funds, assuming no recapture of investment and profit for two and three quarters years.

Generally, Model B involves the acquisition of low-rent units in relatively small buildings that require more extensive rehabilitation than Model A buildings. This is reflected in the high sales price/rent ratio of the converted units when they come on the market. Model B developers borrow a greater proportion of the funds needed for projects than Model A developers. The need for extensive rehabilitation and the concomitant difficulty of achieving a high number of presales indicate that the Model B strategy is high in risk because the developer is subject to cost overruns and time schedule interruptions. The return on investment to the developer, however, is also higher. It is probably this strategy more than any other that results in tenant harassment, partly because tenants are disturbed by extensive rehabilitation work and partly because of the developer's pressing need to sell out quickly to control risk. The Model B strategy probably accounts for less than one quarter of the converted units in our sample.

Model C

Model C characterizes conversion projects undertaken by the landlord of a building. This landlord, however, is not the stereotypical owner of one building. Rather, from our investigations, such an individual is actively involved in the real estate market. This situation is distinctive because building acquisition is not a factor the developer must cope with before undertaking the conversion.

Our data show that for Model C the typical number of units per building was 15; the typical selling price per square foot was $31.00; the typical unit selling price was $34,500; the typical rent before conversion was $350 per month; and the sales price/rent ratio was 100. Landlords who followed this strategy priced their units lower than other developers with respect to selling price and sales price/rent ratio. This possible underpricing holds even when size and rent are held constant. The Model C strategy is much closer to the low price/fast sellout end of the strategy spectrum and may therefore reflect a low risk tolerance on the part of the landlord. While this strategy is similar to that of Model B, the Model C developer is not subject to the same intense financial pressure because the developer makes no new investment of funds to acquire the building. As a result, tenants in the converted building are likely to experience a more relaxed conversion process—that is, less intense pressures to decide quickly to buy or move out.

Data are insufficient to construct a reliable income statement for Model C. We believe only a small proportion of all units have been converted in accordance with this model's strategy.

Summary

The purpose of this chapter has been to describe fully the conversion process as it is carried out by the developer and his financing sources. The risk factors a developer must take into consideration in converting a building are summarized below.

Building Selection.   Has a suitable building been selected for conversion? Has the correct price been paid for it? Will the purchase and sale agreement between the developer and the landlord provide the developer flexibility if presales do not occur? That is, is the purchase and sale agreement an irrevocable contract committing the developer to purchase the building?

Building Rehabilitation.   Has the type of rehabilitation to be undertaken been adequately determined? Has the cost of the rehabilitation been correctly estimated? Have reliable contractors been hired?

Construction of Financial Package.   Is the project adequately capitalized? Will interest expenses be too high? Are the terms of acquisition or rehabilitation loans inflexible? Will potential buyers have assured access to mortgage funds?

Unit Pricing.   Are presale unit prices too high or too low? Are tenant discounts too high or too low? After initial sales, are unit prices too high or too low?

Unit Marketing.   Will units whose characteristics are desirable at the time the building is purchased still be desirable when the units come on the market? Has an adequate target market been identified and reached? What nonprice inducements, if any, should be offered to unit buyers?

Chapter 4

THE EXTENT OF CONDOMINIUM CONVERSION IN BROOKLINE

Condominium conversions in Brookline began in June 1971, when master deeds to convert two buildings were filed. As of late July 1979, 88 buildings, ranging in size from three-family houses to high rise apartment buildings, had been converted. The buildings contain a total of 1,739 units. The vast majority of the 88 buildings are clustered in an area between the MBTA (rapid transit) tracks and Commonwealth Avenue, as shown in Figure 4.1. The concentration of converted units in the northern area of Brookline is attributable to the large number of apartment buildings in this area. Conversions occur most often in apartment buildings.

Characteristics of Condominium Units

The size and purchase price of the converted condominium units varied considerably. The smallest unit converted contained less than 300 square feet in area, whereas the largest unit contained over 4000 square feet. All types of units—from efficiencies to penthouses—are covered in this range. The purchase price of converted units also showed a wide variation. The least expensive unit in Brookline was purchased for $8,000 whereas the most expensive unit was purchased for more than $150,000. Table 4.1 shows the distribution of unit pur-

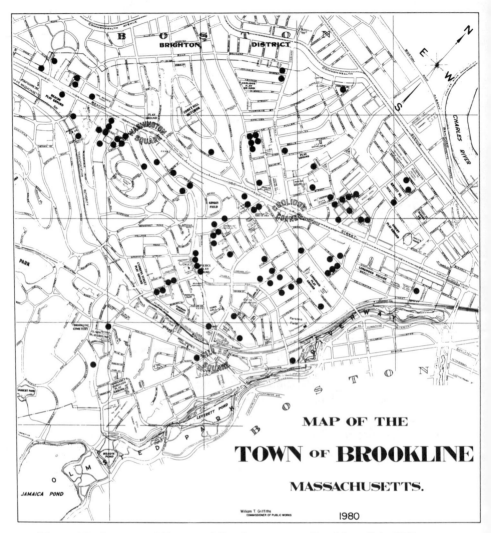

Figure 4.1   Location of Converted Condominiums in Brookline, July 1979.

Table 4.1 Purchase Price of Converted Condominium Units

Price Range of Converted Units	% of Households	No. of Households
$10,000–19,999	4	9
$20,000–29,999	26	62
$30,000–39,999	37	89
$40,000–49,999	22	54
$50,000–59,999	5	12
$60,000–69,999	5	11
$70,000+	3	6
TOTAL	100	243

Source: Harbridge House, Inc., telephone survey data.

chase prices among the condominium owners interviewed in our survey.[1] The average converted unit in Brookline sold between January 1, 1977 and August 1, 1979 had two bedrooms, contained 1091 square feet, and was sold for $39,664, with an average price per square foot of $36.36.

The number of units converted annually to condominiums has fluctuated considerably from year to year, as shown in Table 4.2. Condominium conversion began in 1971 at a modest rate, but in 1972 the rate of conversion more than doubled. The period 1973–1976 was marked by a significant decline in both absolute and relative rates of conversion, due largely to the 1974–1975 recession and its effects on the real estate market. In 1977 this trend reversed sharply as the number of conversions approached the 1973 level. Conversions increased greatly in 1978 as more than 800 apartments were converted to condominiums and continued at about the same rate during the first half of 1979.

A more detailed picture of recent activity in the condominium market is shown in Table 4.3 and Figure 4.2, which present the number of condominium sales on a bimonthly basis from January 1978 to September 1979. While the month-to-month trend is uneven, showing a peak in the fall of 1978, the overall trend since 1971 has been sharply upward.

[1] A total of 293 condominium owners were interviewed, representing about 17 percent of all converted units. The survey methodology is described in Appendix B.

Table 4.2   Annual Rate of Condominium Conversion in Brookline, 1970–1979

Year	No. of Buildings Converted	No. of Units Converted	Annual % Increase in Condominiums
1971	5	71	—
1972	8	149	210
1973	5	121	55
1974	4	73	21
1975	3	15	4
1976	1	4	1
1977	6	113	26
1978	34	808	148
1979 (Jan.–July)	22	385	—
TOTAL	88	1739	—

Source: Harbridge House, Inc., based on records of Brookline Town Assessor's Office.

Table 4.3   Monthly Rate of Condominium Unit Sales in Brookline, January 1978–September 1979

	Month	No. of Units Sold
1978	January	19
	March	16
	May	16
	July	27
	August	34
	September	74
	November	84
1979	January	58
	March	68
	May	57
	July	88
	August	138
	September	124

Source: Harbridge House, Inc., derived from weekly editions of "Banker and Tradesman," Warren, Gorham and Lamont, Inc., Boston, Mass.

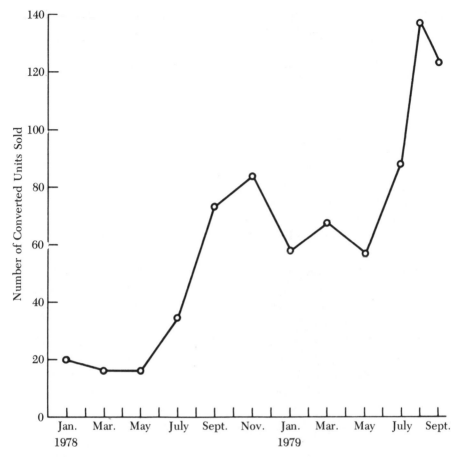

Figure 4.2 Monthly Unit Sales of Brookline Condominiums, January 1978–September 1979.

Converted Buildings Compared with Non-Converted Buildings

According to Rent Control Board records, as of 1979 there were about 11,000 units in Brookline in about 1,070 buildings which were under rent control or had been under rent control before they were converted. As noted, 88 of these buildings, containing 1,739 units, had been converted to condominiums as of July 1979. These buildings represent 15–16 percent of the original rent controlled stock.

How do the converted buildings compare to nonconverted ones in

Table 4.4   Distribution of Units by Numbers of Bedrooms, Rent Controlled Units vs. Converted Units

	Rent Controlled		Converted	
No. of Bedrooms	*Percent*	*Number*	*Percent*	*Number*
Efficiency	5	441	2	9
1	38	3244	38	244
2	41	3490	41	263
3	16	1319	19	124
TOTAL	100	8494°	100	640°

Source: Harbridge House, Inc., based on Town of Brookline Rent Control Board data.
° Excludes units of three bedrooms or more and lodging houses. See Appendix C for more detail.

terms of size and rents? Table 4.4 shows that in terms of number of bedrooms, the proportion of units of different sizes in converted and nonconverted buildings was very similar. For instance, there was about the same proportion of one-bedroom units among the 1,739 condominiums as among the rent controlled apartments.

When comparing building size as opposed to unit size, however, notable differences appear. There were on average 9.5 units in rent controlled buildings and on average 19.8 units in converted buildings. There are two explanations for this difference. Many condominiums counted for property tax purposes as one building (because a single master deed has been filed) were previously operated as several separate rental buildings. The developer chose to convert them as a single condominium. As described in Chapter 3, a developer can obtain financing advantages and cost savings by converting several buildings as a group rather than individually. Second—again because of economies of scale—the most active developers in Brookline prefer to convert larger rather than smaller buildings.

An important difference between converted and non-converted buildings in our sample was in their rent range. Comparing the distribution of pre-conversion rents of converted units with the distribution of rents in current rent controlled apartments, it is evident that higher-priced rental units are more attractive candidates for conversion.[2] These data are shown in Table 4.5. The same pattern is evident when average building rents are compared, as shown in Table 4.6.

---

[2] The data for rents of rent controlled units are based on a tabulation prepared for us by the town of Brookline, shown in Appendix C.

Table 4.5 Distribution of Units by Rent Category, Rent Controlled Units vs. Converted Units

	Rent Controlled		Converted	
Rent Category°	Percent	Number	Percent	Number
Low	17	1453	18	117
Medium	55	4714	32	208
High	28	2327	50	315
TOTAL	100	8494	100	640

Source: Harbridge House, Inc., based on Town of Brookline Rent Control Board data.
° Units included are all those in Brookline Rent Control Board files. Rent ranges for different size units are as defined in Appendix C. "Low" is categories 1 and 2, "medium" is categories 3 and 4, and "high" is categories 5 and 6.

Table 4.6 Distribution of Buildings by Rent Category, Rent Controlled Buildings vs. Converted Buildings

	Rent Controlled		Converted	
Rent Category°	Percent	Number	Percent	Number
Low	28	247	20	6
Medium	55	484	54	16
High	17	149	26	8
TOTAL	100	880	100	30

Source: Harbridge House, Inc., based on Town of Brookline Rent Control Board data.
° Units included are all those in Brookline Rent Control Board files. Rent ranges for different size units are as defined in Appendix C. "Low" is categories 1 and 2, "medium" is categories 3 and 4, and "high" is categories 5 and 6.

In summary, the following facts and generalizations can be presented about condominium conversion in Brookline.

- Since conversion began in 1971, 1,739 units, or 15–16 percent of all rent controlled units, had been converted by July 1979.
- Condominium units were located predominantly in buildings in the northern part of Brookline.
- The rate of building conversions and of unit sales increased greatly during late 1978 and early 1979. Generally, relatively large buildings with relatively high rents had been converted, although individual units were generally the same size as in nonconverted buildings.
- Most condominiums sold were in the $20,000–50,000 range.
- The average (mean) converted unit had two bedrooms, contained about 1100 square feet, and cost $39,664.

Chapter 5

EXPERIENCES OF
KEY PARTICIPANTS

The conversion process often creates an adversary relationship between developers and many of the tenants in apartment houses undergoing conversion. There are two general reasons for this conflict: the attachment of tenants to their renter status and to their place of residence and the need of developers to move out nonbuying tenants to make room for condominium purchasers. This chapter explores the perceptions, attitudes and experiences of all of the parties to this process: post-conversion owners, post-conversion tenants (persons who still rent apartments in converted buildings), displaced tenants, and developers.

Survey Methodology

Almost all of the data in this chapter and Chapter 6 are derived from a detailed survey administered to a sample of Brookline residents. The questionnaire was designed to elicit data about the size, age, income, and composition of households; the marital status, employment status and occupation of the heads of households, spouses, or other adults; about length of residency in Brookline and length of previous and future residencies; and about housing costs. Separate questionnaires were administered to households living in rent controlled units (including converted and unconverted buildings); to households owning and living in converted condominiums; and to households of tenants who had been displaced by conversion. The questionnaires are presented in Appendix A.

A total of 1206 interviews was conducted, each lasting an average of fifteen minutes. The total includes 807 renters living in rent controlled units, 84 renters in converted buildings, 293 condominium owners/occupants, and 22 former tenants who had been displaced by conversion. Except for the displaced tenants, all interviewees were drawn from a random sample of street/telephone number listings for Brookline. Displaced tenants were identified through the efforts of various citizens, coordinated through the Brookline Selectmen's Condominium Study Committee.

After data gathering was completed, the samples of renter and owner households were tested and found generally representative of, respectively, all renter households living in rent controlled apartments in Brookline and all condominium owner/occupant households in Brookline. The 891 renter households constituted 9–10 percent of the roughly 9,000 rent controlled apartments remaining in Brookline as of July 1979. The 293 condominium owners' households constituted 16–17 percent of the 1,600–1,700 occupied condominiums in Brookline as of the same date. These samples are large enough to assure that errors are within a range of ±6 percent for condominium owner households and ±3 percent for renter households. A more detailed description of the survey methodology and of the tests of reliability applied is contained in Appendix B.

Factors Influencing Developer-Tenant Relations

Chapter 3 considered the financial risks and profit incentives that guide developers as they attempt to convert apartment buildings into condominiums. These risks and incentives can be briefly summarized here. Chronologically, a developer's first desire is to secure presales. Commitments to purchase units are the most solid collateral a developer can have in obtaining financing for conversion. If a developer can guarantee the sale of at least 50 percent of the units at the time of seeking bank financing, most banks participating in the conversion market will finance the conversion. Thus the developer's initial strategy will be to woo existing tenants, the most direct way of obtaining these commitments. Thus, initially tenants are likely to experience considerable pressure to buy, including promises of additional renovations, price discounts for prompt purchase commitments, and assistance with financing. These practices are documented in the telephone sample responses analyzed below.

Developers' Incentives

Once the physical conversion process is under way, most developers are anxious to sell out all units as fast as possible. Delay is costly. Interest charges on the condominium mortgage, finance charges on short-term loans for construction (which may be separate from the mortgage), rental income losses from vacant units not yet sold or perhaps not yet renovated, and the opportunity cost of not having the income from unit sales—all are real costs that increase cumulatively over time. Most, though not all, developers find that the best way to control these costs is to sell quickly. (If condominium prices are rising rapidly, however, some developers may prefer to sell units more slowly to take advantage of escalating prices.) Tenants who appear uninterested in purchasing are therefore likely to feel increasing pressure from the developer to vacate their units as time goes on. The experiences of such tenants are described below.

The developer is almost in a Dr. Jekyll and Mr. Hyde situation: Up to a certain point, he will pursue tenants assiduously to get them to purchase; but once it becomes clear that a particular tenant will not buy, the developer usually has strong incentives to try to get that person to move out. Reflection will suggest that tenants acting as a group can potentially exercise a good deal of power during the conversion process. An individual tenant has relatively little leverage with the developer once the tenant has decided not to buy, and whatever leverage he or she has must be exercised fairly quickly. But if all the tenants in a building unite, they may obtain considerable bargaining power with the developer. In Brookline, two instances of this phenomenon were identified. In one instance, the tenants of a small building, acting as a group, purchased the building from the developer at a price that translated into a unit cost significantly lower than the units' current market price. In another instance, the tenants of a large luxury building organized to convince the developer to make substantial improvements in common areas before they would consider purchasing their units. Both examples illustrate clearly that a bargaining relationship can exist between tenants and developers during the conversion process. Individual tenants, however, are usually in a poor position to bargain aggressively, and this is undoubtedly one major source of their complaints against developers.

The adversary relationship between tenant and developer is likely to be exacerbated in the following situations: The developer has little equity in the building and has borrowed a great deal to finance the conversion; rehabilitation costs are high either by design or because of construction problems; the building is low priced and is populated by low-income tenants who are unlikely to be able to buy or to be interested in buying. The tenant/developer relationship is likely to be more harmonious in the following situations: The developer has substantial financial assets and can afford some delays in selling out; the developer has a substantial stake elsewhere in the Brookline housing market so that a bad reputation may damage his other business interests; the units are high priced and in a luxury building, whose tenants are, as a rule, far more likely to buy than less well off tenants.

Tenants' Interests

Our telephone survey revealed that some tenants have strong attachments to their apartments. The strength of their attachments is closely related to their resistance to being moved out by the conversion process and their resentment about having to even consider the possibility of having to move. When renters were asked whether they planned to move from their apartments in the near future, 67 percent of the sample said no. Among persons over 61 this response rose to 78 percent, and even in the under-30 age group—the group with the shortest tenure in apartments—the figure was 63 percent, as shown in Table 5.1. Only among upper income tenants was there a substantial expectation of moving.

The satisfactions tenants derive from their present apartments were the subject of another question, What are the three things you like most about your present apartment? The most common answers had to do with the location of the apartment. Fifty-one percent of respondents cited the neighborhood and 47 percent cited proximity to public transportation as the most attractive feature of their apartment. An attractive rent level was mentioned next most frequently: Thirty-two percent of the sample, including a large number of young people sharing apartments, said the rental was affordable. Among the 84 households (9 percent of the total sample) with school-age children,

Table 5.1 Intentions of Renters in Controlled Units Concerning Moving in the Near Future

	No. Respondents	Intend to Move	Do Not Intend to Move	Do Not Know
Age:				
30 and under	413	28%	63%	9%
31–40	177	24	64	11
41–50	56	18	73	9
51–60	44	11	71	18
61–70	93	11	78	11
71 and over	93	12	71	16
Refused to Answer	14	14	57	29
Income:				
Under $10,000	197	21	68	10
$10,000–$19,999	319	18	72	10
$20,000–$39,999	179	30	62	7
$40,000 and over	30	43 .	44	13
Refused to Answer	163	18	65	17
TOTAL	891	22%	67%	11%

37 percent cited good town schools as an important source of satisfaction with their apartments.

Overall, a good many tenants have a fairly clear idea about why they like their present apartments. It should be expected, therefore, that facing the unwanted prospect of having to choose between moving out or buying would be upsetting. This is particularly true because, as the income/rent analysis in Chapter 6 demonstrates, many tenants could not afford to buy their units if their buildings were converted. Thus the prospect of conversion offers no desirable options to many tenants.

Tenants' Reactions to Prospective Conversions. Predictably, the reactions of tenants whose buildings were candidates for conversion were often quite negative. Of the 165, or 19 percent, of the tenants who said they had heard of possible plans to convert their buildings, only 6 percent had a positive reaction to this news. Another 15 percent had a mixed reaction, and 79 percent had a negative reaction. When all of the interviewees were presented with a choice about the future status of their buildings, most said they would choose to stay as renters. The question asked presented renters with three options: (1) consider purchasing the unit, (2) prefer to stay as a tenant under the protection of the current eviction ban, or (3) move. Only 9 percent said they would consider purchasing; 19 percent said they would move. The rest preferred to stay as tenants. The most favorable reactions to purchasing were among the more affluent respondents, those making $40,000 or more (23 percent) and among those in the 31–40 age group (16 percent). (See Table 5.2.)

Among the large majority of respondents who preferred to stay in their apartments, increasing age and decreasing income were most positively correlated with this preference: Older people and people with incomes under $10,000 were least desirous of moving or buying. Among persons who said they would move, the youngest and the most affluent—those most mobile and most financially able to move—were the most likely to express this preference. (See Table 5.3.)

Approximately 40 percent of the renters who said they would move rather than stay as tenants or buy their units gave as their reason that if their apartments were converted to condominiums they would be "too expensive" for them. Another 20 percent said they simply did not want to own a condominium. Only 5 percent said they were too old to own a condominium or that their buildings had too many problems for them to consider remaining in them as condominium owners. Persons earning more than $40,000 annually were much more likely to point to problems in their buildings as the reason they would move out rather than consider buying. The greater range of ownership choices open to higher income respondents may have produced their greater concern with the quality of the building in which they would choose to own a condominium. A majority of the respondents (53 percent), however, said there were no conditions under which they would consider purchasing their units. Another 20 percent reported a willingness to consider purchasing if their units were offered to them at a comparatively inexpensive, or "reasonable," price. Renovations would prompt a purchase consideration for only 8 percent.

In sum, the most frequent reaction of renters to the prospect of their buildings being converted was unfavorable. It appears that this reaction was based in part on an unfavorable view of condominiums, whether because of cost or other factors, and in part on the feeling that conversion might well force them to move from apartments they had substantial reasons for wanting to stay in.

There was, nevertheless, a significant core of people, generally rela-

Table 5.2 Preference of Households Living in Rent Controlled Building If Building Were Converted, in Relation to Households' Annual Income

Preferences	Income					Total Responses for All Households (%/No.)
	Less than $10,000	$10,000–$19,999	$20,000–$39,999	$40,000+	Income Not Given	
Consider Purchasing	4%	7%	16%	23%	7%	9% (80)
Stay as Tenant	66	68	53	43	62	62 (553)
Move Out	21	18	20	27	16	19 (169)
Do Not Know	9	7	11	7	15	10 (89)
Total Percentages by Income Group	100%	100%	100%	100%	100%	100%
Number (N) of Households in Each Income Group	(N=197)	(N=319)	(N=179)	(N=30)	(N=163)	(N=891)

Table 5.3 Preference of Households Living in Rent Controlled Building If Building Were Converted, in Relation to Respondents' Age

Preferences	30 & Under	31–40	41–50	51–60	61–70	71+	Age Not Given	Total Responses for All Households (%/No.)
				Age				
Consider Purchasing	9%	16%	5%	7%	5%	2%	–	9% (80)
Stay as Tenant	59	56	65	66	66	76	65	62 (553)
Move Out	24	16	14	20	14	11	21	19 (169)
Do Not Know	8	12	16	7	15	11	14	10 (89)
Total Percentage by Age Group	100%	100%	100%	100%	100%	100%	100%	100%
Number (N) Respondents in Each Age Group	(N=413)	(N=177)	(N=56)	(N=44)	(N=93)	(N=93)	(N=14)	(N=891)

tively affluent longer-term residents, who saw conversion of their buildings as desirable. It is such people who, as noted in Chapter 3, are most likely to stay in Brookline as condominium owners and to whom a developer is most likely to be able to make a successful appeal. Because this group is a minority (20–25 percent), however, the relations between developers and the majority of tenants is likely to be antagonistic. This antagonism lays the groundwork for the upsetting experiences some tenants have during the conversion process. Such experiences are analyzed in the following section.

Renters' Experiences with Conversion

Recognizing that a great deal of public attention in Brookline had been focused on the relationships of tenants and developers preceding or during conversion, we made extensive efforts to gather information from Brookline residents about these relationships. Many questions were asked of current renters in both converted and nonconverted buildings, and a small number of former Brookline residents displaced by conversion were interviewed as well.

Renters Living in Converted and Unconverted Buildings

For the purposes of the following analysis, our sample of 891 renters was divided between those who lived in converted buildings (84) and those who did not (807).[1] The interview questionnaire contained 23 questions directed explicitly at the tenant's experience with what is often termed landlord harassment. The results are summarized on Table 5.4. Because many of the numbers presented in this table are small, percentage rounding errors would obscure a good deal of information. Therefore, actual numbers of responses are shown.

Except for landlords' petitions for rent increases and parking fee increases, which may have had nothing to do with the landlords' intentions regarding conversion, relatively few tenants reported having

---

[1] There was some discrepancy between those who said their buildings had been converted when asked—only 66—and the record of buildings actually converted. Telephone interviews were completed with 84 respondents whose telephone numbers were listed as being in converted buildings. It is these 84 respondents who were coded on the questionnaire as living in converted buildings and who are so analyzed here.

Table 5.4   **Experiences of Renters in Converted and Unconverted Buildings with the Conversion Process**

Question[*]	Renters in Unconverted Buildings (N=807)		Renters in Converted Buildings (N=84)	
	Yes	No	Yes	No
13. Has landlord tried to harass you because he wanted to convert your unit?	14 (2%)	793 (98%)	8 (10%)	71 (90%)
12. Has owner tried to evict you so building could be converted?	20 (2%)	781 (97%)	5 (6%)	79 (94%)
If yes to question 12, answer 14–19.				
14. How much time were you given to vacate?				
less than 1 week	—		1	
1 week to 1 month	5		1	
more than 1 month	6		1	
15. Were you given adequate advance notice?	3	11	2	2
19. Did landlord cause trouble after giving notice to vacate?	7	11	3	2
21. Has landlord petitioned for rent increases in last 12 months?	547 (68%)	177 (22%)	44 (52%)	25 (30%)
If yes to question 21, answer 22–23.				
22. What was amount of increase?				
$10–50 per month	379 (69%)		25 (57%)	
over $50 per month	77 (14%)	—	10 (23%)	—
23. Was increase granted?	462 (84%)	86 (16%)	30 (68%)	12 (27%)
For those with parking space, answer 25–26.				
25. Has landlord tried to take your parking space away?	17 (5%)	347 (95%)	5 (9%)	48 (91%)
26. Has landlord tried to increase parking fee in last 12 months?	180 (49%)	176 (48%)	15 (28%)	38 (72%)
27. Has landlord made improvements in last 12 months that you did not request?	118 (15%)	666 (83%)	19 (23%)	62 (74%)
29. Has landlord cut back on services in last 12 months?	108 (13%)	680 (84%)	14 (17%)	68 (81%)

Table 5.4 **Experiences of Renters in Converted and Unconverted Buildings with the Conversion Process** (*cont.*)

Question*	Renters in Unconverted Buildings (N=807)		Renters in Converted Buildings (N=84)	
	Yes	*No*	*Yes*	*No*
30. If yes to question 29, which services?				
garbage pickup	22		6	
building maintenance	33		2	
heat	29		2	
all other	24		4	
31. Has landlord attempted to sell your apartment as condominium?	37 (5%)	685 (85%)	14 (17%)	60 (71%)
32. Has he brought prospective buyers to see your apartment?	18	24	7	7
33. If yes to question 32, how much notice did he give you?				
less than 1 day	11		2	
more than 1 day	3		2	
34. If yes to question 32, how many times?				
1 or 2	6		1	
3 or more	12		5	

* See Appendix A for complete text of questions.

experienced anything that might be termed harassment. On most questions, only a few percent of respondents stated that their landlords had committed acts that might be deemed harassment. Tenants reported cutbacks in services by landlords somewhat more often (13 percent), but such actions are not necessarily related to prospective conversions. A significant number of respondents (15 percent) reported their landlords had made physical improvements they had not requested, but again there is no reason to believe that these actions constituted harassment. The overall pattern of the individual responses is consistent with responses to the direct question of whether the landlord had engaged in harassment: To this question, only 2 percent of respondents answered yes.

As opposed to the low number of tenants reporting landlord harassment, a significant majority of the respondents (69 percent) reported that their landlords had petitioned to have their rent increased during the preceding twelve months. In 84 percent of the cases, the tenants reported that the petition had been granted. Discussions with Rent Control Board personnel indicate that both of these percentages are higher than those their records indicate, suggesting that tenants may not have been aware that some rent increases resulted from general increases granted by the board to all landlords. The average monthly increase granted was usually reported to be in the range of ten to fifty dollars per month. In addition, nearly half (49 percent) of the tenants who had parking spaces reported that their landlords had raised the fee for these spaces during the preceding twelve months.

It should be recognized, in interpreting these figures, that the reported rent and parking fee increases come from a percentage of all renters in the sample (891), whereas the relatively few reports of harassment came from a percentage of the small number of households whose buildings were involved in the conversion process. It may be that only the 100 households (12 percent) that reported hearing of plans to convert their buildings were in a situation in which conversion was imminent or under way.

The experiences of tenants in converted buildings, however, was not significantly different from that of tenants in non-converted buildings. Tenants in converted buildings did experience a higher level of intrusions from prospective buyers, which is to be expected. On the other hand, their landlords were less likely to try to raise their rents or their parking fees. Overall, it would appear that the awareness of developer harassment related to the conversion process was quite low among current renters, whether they lived in converted or nonconverted buildings. The experiences of persons actually displaced by the conversion process however, was much more unpleasant, as is described below.

Condominium Owners Purchasing Previously Rented Units

A significant number (68, or 23 percent) of condominium owners interviewed had rented the units they owned or had rented other units in the same building. Persons in this group were asked about their relations with their former landlords during the conversion process. Among these former renters, 19 percent said the landlords had applied some pressure on them to purchase. When asked to be specific, about 10 percent identified the landlords' tactics as bringing in prospective buyers or renovating the units while they occupied them. The former renter group was also asked about how good a job the developers had done in rehabilitating the units and the buildings for sale as condominiums. While our tabulations do not permit direct analysis of the answers, the distribution of positive responses suggest that although there was a high level of satisfaction with the quality of developers' work among members of this group, approval was not universal.

Renters Displaced by Conversion

Most displaced tenants, as might be expected, had very negative reactions about having been forced to move because of condominium conversion. Respondents expressed feelings of anger and frustration at having had to change long-established living arrangements or at having had to bear the expense and trouble of moving. Of the 22 respondents, 16, or 73 percent, had negative reactions to their moves. Of the 6 respondents who expressed either neutral or positive reactions, all had had other reasons for moving. Even though in all but one case the owners had required them to move, these respondents either already had had a place to move to or had planned to leave anyway. In three cases, the families had owned second homes and seemed satisfied to have moved to them. In two cases, families had already made plans to move, and in one case, the move simply created no particular hardship or negative feeling.

But the reactions of the other 16 displaced tenants were strong and negative. Typical comments included: "It was traumatic to be forced to move twice in five years because of condominiums." "I felt like a lost person . . . at loose ends for several months living out of a suitcase." "Very upsetting. I lived there 23 years; I had to deal with aggravation and harassment which had a great deal of effect on me economically and healthwise." "We felt manipulated by forces beyond our control." "It infuriated me. It is hard for a single person to find the time to look for a place. The cost was exorbitant—about $1000 to move."

How did the conversion process, from beginning to end, affect displaced tenants? From the time they became aware that their apartments were to be converted to the time they settled into new residences, what can be said about the experiences of these former tenants?

Only half of the tenants we interviewed first heard about the impending conversion directly from their landlords; the other half got the news indirectly—from neighbors, by rumor, and the like. Their unanimous reaction to the news was, predictably, displeasure, ranging from "surprise" to "utter outrage." Many had suspected that plans for conversion had been under way for some time (our analysis in Chapter 3 bears this out) and were resentful that they hadn't been notified earlier. Those who heard the news only by rumor had difficulty getting anyone in authority to confirm the information—an additional source of frustration to them.

Six of the 22 respondents said they had been given between one week and one month to find a new place to live, 2 said less than one week, 2 said between one and six months, and 12 reported no specific time frame. Only 3 respondents received offers of help in relocating from their landlords, but they did not receive (and perhaps did not ask for) any specific help.

Finding a new place to live was reported to be "very difficult" for 12 respondents, "not at all difficult" for 6, and between the two extremes for 4. The chief difficulties reported were those of finding a reasonable rent and a good location. The average time needed to find a new apartment was about three months, with actual times ranging from less than one week (3) to more than six months (5). Twelve of the tenants found a new residence in Brookline, 6 elsewhere in the greater Boston area, 3 elsewhere in Massachusetts, and 1 out of state. It should be noted, however, that this distribution is very much a function of the accuracy and completeness of the records available. These records are more likely to be accurate for persons who have stayed in Brookline and have kept in touch with former neighbors. In cases in which records were incomplete, the person in question could not be reached.

What actual pressures did building owners bring on non-purchasing tenants to move? In our sample, the owner was most probably the developer, not the unit purchaser. Although 12 former tenants reported that their units had been sold before they moved out, it appears likely that they still dealt with developers rather than unit owners. This observation is based on the responses of condominium owners. While 57 percent (168) of the owners said their units were still occupied when they bought them, no one said they had to deal directly with the tenants. The tenants either moved out, or the developer handled the situation. Perhaps somewhat surprisingly, only 6 of the 22 displaced tenants reported that the owner "caused trouble" after giving them notice to vacate. The "trouble" mainly appeared to consist of lack of service and inadequate building maintenance. About the same proportion of tenants, 6 out of 22, reported that the landlord had cut back on some kinds of service during the preceding twelve months.

Petitions for rent increases were reported quite frequently as a form of landlord action. Seventeen former tenants reported that their landlords had petitioned for rent increases during the preceding twelve months. Of these, 14 respondents said the inceases had been granted. Nine of these increases were from ten to fifty dollars per month and 4 were over fifty dollars a month. This proportion of rent increase petitions is, however, comparable to that for all current renters, as reported above.

Why did these non-purchasing tenants finally leave their apartments? Four reported some form of court action involving their landlords which was unfavorable to them, in some cases actions the tenants initiated. (These actions took place prior to Brookline's enactment of a ban on conversion-related evictions.) Four said the prices asked for their units were too high, and 8 said they did not want to own a condominium. One respondent thought a condominium was a poor investment.

The overall feeling that emerges is one of strong hostility of displaced tenants towards landlords, hostilities that grew up as the interests of the two parties clashed. From our small sample of responses, it appears that these angry feelings were more directly engendered by being forced to move rather than by overt acts of building owners. This hostility is more readily understandable when it is recognized that 9 of the 22 respondents had lived in their units over five years, and 6 more had lived in their units from two to five years.

When the displaced tenants were finally resettled, what was their reaction? Despite the trauma these tenants suffered as a result of their forced relocation—or perhaps because of it—17 said their new residences were better (15) or the same as (2) the places they had had to leave. Four now live in homes they bought or previously owned, 2 live in condominiums, and the rest rent. Respondents generally had positive feelings about their new residences even though the residences rented for more and were smaller (in total space, not in number of bedrooms) than the former units. The median rent for the group went up about 5 percent, from $382 to $403.[2]

---

[2] The small sample size may have produced some distortion here, however: A number of interviewees had significantly higher rents, although a few had lower rents. Higher rents were specifically mentioned by about one quarter of the sample.

Condominium Owners' Experiences with Condominium Purchase

A number of aspects of new condominium owners' experiences in purchasing condominiums have been reported above. In Chapter 2 we noted that many purchasers considered other types of housing before buying condominiums. The average search period for owners' present residence was four to six months, with about half settling on their final purchase in six months or less. Chapter 3 described the types of financial inducements developers are likely to offer tenants to achieve their target of presales. Among tenants who purchased condominiums, about half (43 percent) were offered these inducements and half were not.

Previously in this chapter we noted that most purchasers seemed satisfied with the work developers had done on the units and the buildings. About 18 percent, however, said they were dissatisfied with work on either the units or the buildings. A somewhat higher proportion of dissatisfaction occurred among former renters in buildings than among first-time residents. Dissatisfaction arose from such things as poor workmanship and failure of developers to make all promised improvements, such as repairing roofs and putting in intercom systems. A relatively high proportion of owners (31 percent) also said the actual costs of ownership were higher than the developer had said they would be.

In general, however, despite some complaints about higher costs and faulty or incomplete rehabilitation work, there seems substantial satisfaction among condominium owners with their purchases. For instance, among the 13 percent of owners who said they planned to move during the next three years very few cited dissatisfaction with their condominiums as the reason. Less than ten respondents said that the reason they were planning to move was that carrying costs were too high.

One other potential source of difficulty in the conversion process is friction between unit owners and renters who remain in unsold units. About one third of the owners, 94 respondents, lived in buildings that also housed persons who rented unsold units. Of these 94, two thirds said that the renters created no problems. The remaining third, 30 respondents, cited a variety of reactions to this situation, ranging from irritation that the tenants would not move, to complaints that the tenants did not participate in paying the common area charges, to the impression that "tenants and owners are different types who don't mix well."

Summary

We have reviewed the experiences of all parties involved in the conversion process—that is, the experiences of people as they buy, sell, move into, or move out of residence units in an apartment building that is being converted into a condominium. On balance, it appears that no more than about 20 percent of the respondents had any type of unpleasant experience with conversion. Almost all of the displaced tenants had highly unsettling experiences, of course, but we cannot estimate accurately what proportion these persons represent in Brookline's entire rental population, although the figure is surely well under 10 percent. When condominium owners' reactions to developers' performance are compared with renters' detection of landlord harassment, we note a significantly higher proportion of condominium owners (about 20 percent) reported dissatisfaction with developers. This statistic suggests that condominium purchasers also need some form of protection in the conversion process.

It should be noted that our survey was in no way an opinion poll. It was not an effort to query a cross section of Brookline residents about whether they liked the idea of condominium conversion. Our questionnaires sought specific information about respondents' direct involvement in various aspects of the conversion process. On balance, conversion was an unpleasant experience for only a small minority of the 1206 Brookline residents we interviewed.

Chapter 6

CHANGES IN BROOKLINE'S POPULATION RESULTING FROM CONVERSION

A principal focus of the preceding analysis has been on the involvement of individuals in the conversion process: how a developer converts a building; who buys the converted units; how the conversion process affects renters and owners. In this chapter and in Chapter 7 we turn to the aggregate effects of conversion: how the character of a town's population changes as owners replace renters and how the town's fiscal condition changes as condominiums replace rental units.

Large-scale conversion raises significant issues of public policy only in part because it is seen by some people as an unequal contest between persons with economic power—developers—and persons without economic power—tenants who cannot afford to or do not wish to purchase their apartments. Changing a significant part of a community's housing stock from rental property to condominiums, however, also raises other issues no community can ignore. Is housing being priced out of the reach of many current community residents? As a result, is the character of the community's population changing significantly? And, as a result, is the existing relationship between local property tax revenues and municipal service demands changing?

In this chapter we examine how Brookline renters as a group compare to Brookline condominium owners as a group and as a result how much the town's population is changing due to large-scale conversion. A basis for analyzing the future direction of this change is also provided through an examination of the relationship between income and housing costs for different population groups in Brookline.

Characteristics of Condominium Owners

This section describes the basic characteristics—including age, income, rent, occupation, length of residence, and household size—of our sample of 293 households living in converted condominium units in Brookline. As represented in this sample, Brookline residents living in converted condominium units tend to be in the 30–40 age group, married, and childless and tend to have annual incomes in the $25,000–30,000 range. Most of these residents have professional or managerial jobs. A small but notable group is comprised of persons over sixty, many of whom are retired but who have incomes from interest, dividends, or other sources that are representative of the income of all Brookline condominium owners.

Household Characteristics

The age distribution of households in the sample was multi-modal, as shown in Table 6.1. The largest age cluster was the 31–40 age group. Another cluster in the under-30 age group, and the remainder of residents were distributed among other age groups. To capture this distribution in a form that facilitates analysis, the respondents are grouped in three clusters: under 30, 31–60, and over 60.

The average household size of condominium owners in our sample was 1.95. About 50 percent of the households had only one or two members, and over three quarters had no children, as shown in Table 6.2. There were 100 children in the households included in the sample, comprising 17.9 percent of all people living in these households. There was an average of 0.346 children per household.

Table 6.1 Age Distribution of Condominium Owners

Age	No. of Households	% of Households
30 and Under	70	24
31–40	94	33
41–50	45	15
51–60	36	12
61–70	24	8
71 and Over	19	6
Not Given	5	2
TOTAL	293	100

Table 6.2   Household Size of Condominium Owners

No. of Households	No. of Occupants in Unit	% of Sample
108	1	37
123	2	42
28	3	10
34	4 or more	11
293		100

No. of Households	No. of Adults in Household	Total Adults in Sample
127	1	127
150	2	300
6	3	18
3	4 or more	14
7	NA	–
293		459

No. of Households	No. of Children in Household	Total Children in Sample
229	0	0
28	1	28
24	2	48
8	3	24
4	NA	–
293		100

Total Sample Population: 559

Children per Household: 0.346

Table 6.3   Marital Status of Condominium Owners

Marital Status	No. of Households	% of Households
Married	128	44
Single	102	35
Single Parent	23	8
Widowed/Divorced/Separated	31	10
Not Given	9	3
	293	100

About 44 percent of the households in the sample were married households, and an additional 8 percent were single parent households, as shown in Table 6.3. Thus about 48 percent of the households in the sample were not families in the traditional sense of the term—that is, they lacked two spouses, lacked children, or lacked both.

Table 6.4   **Household Income of Condominium Owners**

Income	No. of Households	% of Households
Under $10,000	8	3
$10,000–19,999	64	22
$20,000–29,999	75	26
$30,000–39,999	41	14
$40,000–49,999	13	4
$50,000 and Over	25	9
Not Given	67	22
TOTAL	293	100

Mean Income: $27,830

In general, condominium owners in the sample were in the upper-to-moderate income range. As shown in Table 6.4, only 25 percent of the sample had incomes below $20,000, and 37 percent had incomes over $30,000. The mean household income was $27,830. About 22 percent of households interviewed did not reveal their incomes.

There is a surprising similarity in the distribution of income by age among all income groups, as shown in Table 6.5. In all three age groups, the spread between lower and higher income brackets is fairly close. People under thirty were more heavily represented in the $10,000–20,000 income group, and people over sixty were somewhat more heavily represented in the $40,000-and-over income group. But in general there is not a strong age/income correlation. This income distribution is probably in part a reflection of the relatively narrow range of most condominium prices in Brookline.

Over three quarters of the sampled households depended on wages or salaries as the primary income source, as shown in Table 6.6. Among respondents over sixty, about one third depended on Social Security or pensions. But an even larger portion of the over-60 group, 37 percent, reported that interest or dividends were the primary source of income, and another 15 percent cited "other" sources of income (a category that excluded public assistance). In other words, the relatively higher income of the over-60 age group reflects a high proportion of households living off substantial accumulated savings.

The preponderance of wage and salary earners was reflected in the over 80 percent of the respondents who were employed. (See Table 6.7.) About 10 percent of the sample was retired and only 8 percent unemployed. Over three quarters of the males and over 60 percent of

Table 6.5 Income of Condominium Owner in Relation to Owner's Age

Age of Respondent	Number of Respondents in Each Age Group	Income					Total Percentage by Age
		Under $10,000	$10,000–19,999	$20,000–29,999	$30,000–39,999	$40,000 and Over	
30 and Under	64	5%	37%	30%	19%	9%	100%
31–60	136	2%	24%	38%	19%	17%	100%
61 and Over	27	7%	27%	22%	11%	33%	100%
Not Given	66						

Total Respondents: 293

Table 6.6 Primary Income Sources of Condominium Owners

Primary Income Source	% of Households
Salary/Wages	78
Interest/Dividends	4
Self-Employed	4
Social Security/Pension	4
Other	4
Not Given	6
TOTAL	100
	(N = 293)

Table 6.7   Occupation of Condominium Owner by Sex of Respondent

Occupational Status	% of Males	% of Females	% of Males & Females
Employed	(85)	(77)	(81)
Professional	65	48	55
Technical	2	2	2
Managerial	13	14	14
Sales	1	3	2
Clerical	1	7	5
Other°	4	3	3
Do Not Know	—	1	1
Not in Labor Force	(13)	(22)	(18)
Retired	9	11	10
Unemployed	5	11	8
Do Not Know	1	1	1
Total Percentage by Sex	100	100	100
Number (N) of Respondents by Sex	(N=119)	(N=174)	(N=293)

Note: Percentages may not total 100 due to rounding.
° "Other" includes craftsmen, equipment operators, transportation workers, laborers, farm workers, and service and household workers.

Table 6.8   Occupation by Sex of Spouse or Other Principal Condominium Household Member

Occupational Status	% of Males	% of Females	% of Males & Females
Employed	(63)	(88)	(75)
Professional	49	53	50
Technical	1	4	3
Managerial	5	22	13
Sales	1	4	3
Clerical	7	0	4
Other°	1	3	2
Do Not Know	0	0	0
Not in Labor Force	(35)	(13)	(17)
Retired	4	8	6
Unemployed	31	5	11
Do Not Know	2	0	1
Total Percentage by Sex	100	100	100
Number (N) of Responses by Sex	(N=78)	(N=72)	(N=150)

Note: Percentages may not total 100 due to rounding.
° "Other" includes craftsmen, equipment operators, transportation workers, laborers, farm workers, and service and household workers.

the females had professional or managerial jobs. Except for a small (7 percent) number of female clerical workers, no other job category was well represented.

In about 38 percent of the households, there were two job holders, either spouses or condominium co-owners. In general, there was a close similarity between the occupation or employment status of respondents (usually heads of households) and their spouses or co-owners, but there were notable differences between the occupation or employment status of the sexes in each group (see Table 6.8). Among spouses or co-owners, the employment rate was slightly lower than among principal household members, but a larger proportion of males than females were unemployed. The overall distribution of types of jobs held was quite similar to that of the respondents, but a larger proportion of females had managerial or professional jobs.

Residency Characteristics

Almost half of the current condominium owners had their previous residence in Brookline, either at the same or a different address. Table 6.9 shows that 22 percent lived at the same address in Brookline and another 27 percent lived elsewhere in Brookline. (Virtually all of those who lived at the same address also lived in the same unit—that is, they bought units they previously rented.) Another 35 percent lived elsewhere in the Boston area, and only 15 percent moved to Brookline from outside the Boston area or from outside Massachusetts. In short, the principal market for Brookline condominiums was, first, persons currently living in the apartments to be converted and other Brookline residents, and second, other Boston-area residents. Many of the latter came from the adjacent Boston communities of Brighton, Cambridge, and Newton.

Since people tend to become less mobile as they get older, it is not surprising that the percentage of people who either bought their apartments when they were converted or moved from elsewhere in Brookline steadily increased from 38 percent for the 30-and-under age group to 51 percent for the 41–50 age group to 62 percent for the 61–70 age group. Among people over 71, 69 percent purchased their previous apartments.

Most of the condominium owners moved from rental units. Seventy-five percent rented apartments, and 6 percent rented homes, as shown

Table 6.9 Previous Residence of Condominium Owner in Relation to Owner's Age

Previous Residence	Age						Total by Residence	
	30 and Under	31–40	41–50	51–60	61–70	71+		
Brookline, Same Address	11%	19%	20%	22%	29%	69%	22%	(69)
Brookline, Different Address	27	23	31	36	33	5	27	(78)
Metro Boston, Outside Brookline	40	47	33	11	34	16	34	(103)
Massachusetts, Outside Metro Boston	11	3	7	17	4	5	8	(22)
Outside Massachusetts	11	7	7	11	—	5	8	(23)
Not Given	—	1	2	3	—	—	1	
Total Percentages by Age Group	100%	100%	100%	100%	100%	100%	100%	
Total Number (N) of Responses by Age Group	(N=70)	(N=94)	(N=45)	(N=36)	(N=24)	(N=19)	(N=290)	

Table 6.10   Type of Previous Residence of Condominium Owner

Type of Previous Residence	% of Households	No. of Households
Owner Occupied House	16	47
Owner Occupied Condominium	2	7
Rental House	6	17
Rental Apartment	75	219
Other	1	3
TOTAL	100	293

in Table 6.10. Of the remainder, 16 percent moved from their own home, and 3 percent moved from another condominium. Thus the majority of Brookline condominium purchasers were first-time homeowners, and the majority previously lived in Brookline.

Over half of the condominiums in our sample were purchased for between $20,000 and $40,000, as shown in Table 6.11, and most of these units were purchased by buyers under forty years of age. The most common pattern in the Brookline condominium market, representing about 40 percent of all sampled households, is that of a person aged forty or under purchasing a $20,000–40,000 unit. The next largest age/price cluster occurs among persons in the 41–60 year age group purchasing $30,000–50,000 units.

The correlation between purchase price and household income is fairly strong, as shown in Table 6.12. Among households with incomes under $20,000, about half paid less than $30,000 for their unit, but among households with incomes over $40,000 about 60 percent bought units costing over $40,000. The most common types of units in the $20,000–30,000 range had one bedroom; in the $30,000–40,000 range, two bedrooms; and in the $40,000–50,000 range, three bedrooms. These three types of units accounted for about 45 percent of all units purchased, as shown in Table 6.13.

Table 6.14 shows the relationship between household income and reported carrying costs for condominiums. Carrying costs include mortgage principal and interest, property taxes, and the maintenance or condominium association fee. As would be expected, there is a fairly strong correlation between household income and level of carrying charges. Almost two thirds of households with incomes under $20,000 paid $500 or less per month, but over two thirds of households with incomes over $50,000 paid over $500 per month. The proportion of income spent on housing declined as income increased, as the following breakdown shows:

Condominium Carrying Cost in Relation to Owner's Income

No. of Households	Household Income	Average Monthly Payments	Payments as % of Income
8	Less than $10,000	$350	56°
64	$10,000–19,999	$445	36
75	$20,000–29,999	$460	22
41	$30,000–39,999	$515	17
13	$40,000–49,999	$545	15
25	$50,000 and Over	$565	12†
226			

Mean Income: $27,830
Mean Monthly Payments: $478
Mean Payment/Income Ratio: 21%

° Assumes an average income of $7,500.
† Assumes an average income of $55,000.

The relationship between age and size of monthly payments is not sharply delineated. Table 6.15 shows, however, that over half of the respondents under 30 paid less than $500 per month and that about half the respondents in the 41–50 age group paid over $500 per month. It is noteworthy that people over 60 were fairly evenly distributed with regard to the size of their monthly payments.

In sum, then, almost half of the Brookline condominium owners in our sample formerly rented in Brookline, and many of the rest rented in neighboring communities. The older condominium owners were, the more likely they were to have rented the unit they purchased. For the large majority of current owners, condominiums were the first homes purchased.

The largest group of units purchased was in the $20,000–40,000 range. These units had one or two bedrooms and typical monthly carrying costs of $400 or less. A significant portion of people sixty and over bought higher-priced units. The average condominium in our sample cost $37,263, and purchasers had an average income of $27,830. On average, purchasers paid $478 a month in carrying costs, or an average of 21 percent of their monthly income.

Principal, Secondary, and Tertiary Household Profiles

As a way of summarizing the types of households that have purchased condominiums in Brookline, it is useful to establish clusters of typical

Table 6.11 Condominium Price in Relation to Purchaser's Age

Price of Unit	30 & Under	31–40	41–50	51–60	61–70	71+	Not Given	Total by Unit Price (%/No.)
$10,000–19,999	6%	3%	2%	3%	–	–%	–	3% (9)
$20,000–29,999	26	23	16	22	21	11	–	21 (62)
$30,000–39,999	39	36	22	30	21	11	20	30 (89)
$40,000–49,999	10	20	36	14	13	21	–	19 (54)
$50,000 and Over	8	6	11	17	8	21	–	10 (29)
Not Given	11	12	13	14	37	36	80	17 (50)
Total Percentage by Age Group	100%	100%	100%	100%	100%	100%	100%	100%
Number (N) of Responses by Age Group	(N=70)	(N=94)	(N=45)	(N=36)	(N=24)	(N=19)	(N=5)	(N=293)

Table 6.12 Condominium Price in Relation to Purchaser's Income

Price of Unit	Under $20,000	$20,000–29,999	$30,000–39,999	$40,000–49,999	$50,000 & Over	Not Given	Total by Unit Price (%/No.)
$10,000–19,999	3%	3%	5%	8%	–	1%	3% (9)
$20,000–29,999	47	26	5	–	16	6	21 (62)
$30,000–39,999	24	42	56	31	12	17	30 (89)
$40,000–49,999	12	23	22	38	16	14	19 (54)
$50,000 and Over	5	3	7	23	48	8	10 (29)
Not Given	9	3	5	–	8	54	17 (50)
Total Percentage by Income Group	100%	100%	100%	100%	100%	100%	100%
Number (N) of Responses by Income Group	(N=72)	(N=75)	(N=41)	(N=13)	(N=25)	(N=65)	(N=293)

Table 6.13 Number of Bedrooms in Condominium Unit in Relation to Unit Price

Price of Unit	No. of Rooms					Total by Unit Price (%/No.)
	Efficiency	One	Two	Three	Four or More	
$10,000–19,999	100%	1%	1%	8%	—	3% (9)
$20,000–29,999	—	44	10	22	25	21 (62)
$30,000–39,999	—	19	41	15	42	30 (89)
$40,000–49,999	—	10	20	29	8	19 (54)
$50,000 and Over	—	—	12	18	8	10 (29)
Not Given	—	26	16	8	17	17 (50)
Total Percentage by Unit Size	100%	100%	100%	100%	100%	100%
Number (N) of Units of Each Size	(N=2)	(N=72)	(N=147)	(N=60)	(N=12)	(N=293)

Table 6.14 Monthly Carrying Cost of Condominium in Relation to Owner's Income

Monthly Carrying Cost	Income						Total of Carrying Cost Groups (%/No.)
	Under $20,000	$20,000–29,999	$30,000–39,999	$40,000–49,999	$50,000 and Over	Not Given	
Less than $400	42%	23%	12%	8%	8%	14%	22% (63)
$400–499	21	36	27	31	20	9	23 (68)
$500–599	17	24	29	8	20	14	19 (57)
$600 or More	3	7	20	46	48	6	14 (40)
Not Given	17	10	12	7	4	57	22 (65)
Total Percentage by Income Category	100%	100%	100%	100%	100%	100%	100%
Number (N) of Respondents in Each Income Category	(N=72)	(N=75)	(N=41)	(N=13)	(N=25)	(N=67)	(N=293)

Table 6.15 Condominium Carrying Cost in Relation to Owner's Age

Monthly Carrying Costs	Age							Total of Carrying Cost Groups (%/No.)
	30 & Under	31–40	41–50	51–60	61–70	70+	Not Given	
Less than $400	26%	15%	18%	39%	20%	16%	—	22% (63)
$400–499	29	33	17	14	8	10	—	23 (68)
$500–599	17	23	22	14	17	26	—	19 (57)
$600 and Over	10	14	27	8	8	11	20	14 (40)
Not Given	18	15	16	25	47	37	80	22 (65)
Total Percentage by Age Group	100%	100%	100%	100%	100%	100%	100%	100%
Number (N) of Respondents in Each Age Group	(N=70)	(N=94)	(N=45)	(N=36)	(N=24)	(N=19)	(N=5)	(N=293)

characteristics. These clusters, or profile groups, represent the three modal types of condominium owners within the overall sample population.

A. *Principal Household Profile*

1. Middle age households whose head is 31–60 years of age; about half are married households; may be termed "midstream families."
2. Mean size 2.09 persons; generally, no children.
3. Average income $28,327 per year.
4. Principal source of income salary or wages, derived from professional or managerial job.
5. Average cost of condominium $36,188; monthly carrying charges $483.
6. About half lived in Brookline before purchasing current condominium.

B. *Secondary Household Profile*

1. Young households whose head is thirty years of age or under. About half are married households; may be termed "young professionals."
2. Mean size 1.86 persons; only a little more likely to have children than principal profile group.
3. Average income $24,961.
4. Principal source of income salary or wages, derived from professional or managerial job.
5. Average cost of condominium $34,355; monthly carrying charges $461.
6. Most moved into Brookline to buy condominium.

C. *Tertiary Household Profile*

1. Older households whose head is sixty-one years of age or over; almost half still married households; may be termed "comfortably retireds."
2. Mean size 1.60 persons; many are single person households.
3. Average income $28,444, although wide dispersion between high and low incomes.
4. Principal source of income interest, dividends, other nonpublic sources (such as support from children), Social Security, or pensions.

5. Average cost of condominium $42,037; monthly carrying charges $458.
6. Most lived in Brookline before purchasing current condominium.

Condominiums in Brookline seem to attract three types of purchasers. First, midstream families—married professional people, in midlife, sometimes with children; second, young professionals, probably unmarried, who are likely to be first-time residents of Brookline; third, retired people in comfortable financial circumstances, often single, who are long-time Brookline residents and are probably owners of apartments they previously rented. These three groups, as identified in our sample, were perhaps more remarkable for their similarities than their differences. Their average incomes were fairly close and were likely to be earned by two wage earners; their propensity to be married was similar, and except for the older group, they were equally likely to have children. What the three groups paid for their condominiums, both originally and in monthly costs, was also fairly similar. In short, it seems likely that the characteristics of condominiums being offered in Brookline—their size, cost, amenities, and location—attract people who, except for their stage of life, are more similar than dissimilar.

Characteristics of Renters

Compared with condominium owners, most of the renters in rent controlled units interviewed for this study tended to be younger, to have lower incomes, and to be a little less likely to hold professional or managerial jobs than condominium owners. Older renters were more likely to be living alone than condominium owners of similar ages and were likely to have significantly lower income levels.

Household Characteristics

The age distribution of the 891 renter households in the sample was roughly trimodal, with the largest concentration under thirty years of age and other noticeable concentrations in the 31–40 and over-60 categories. (See Table 6.16). The average household size among renters was 2.05 persons. These households were slightly larger on average than the 1.95 average of the condominium owner population. (See

Table 6.16   Age Distribution of Renters in Controlled Units

Age	No. of Households	% of Households
30 and Under	413	47
31–40	177	20
41–50	56	6
51–60	44	5
61–70	93	10
71 and Over	93	10
Not Given	14	2
TOTAL	890	100

Table 6.17   Household Size of Renters in Controlled Units

No. of Households	No. of Occupants in Apartment	% of Sample
319	1	36
336	2	38
123	3	14
103	4 or more	11
10	NA	1
891		100%

No. of Households	No. of Adults in Household	Total Adults in Sample
351	1	351
386	2	772
92	3	276
42	4	168
9	5	45
11	NA	—
891		1,612

No. of Households	No. of Children in Household	Total Children in Sample
762	0	0
64	1	64
50	2	100
8	3	24
891		188

Total Sample Population: 1,800
Children Per Household: 0.214

Table 6.18 **Marital Status of Renters in Controlled Units**

Marital Status	No. of Households	% of Households
Married	239	27
Single	480	54
Single Parent	42	5
Widowed/Divorced/Separated	108	12
Not given	22	2
TOTAL	891	100

Table 6.19 **Household Income of Renters in Controlled Units**

Income	No. of Households	% of Households
Under $10,000	197	22
$10,000–19,999	319	36
$20,000–29,999	141	16
$30,000–39,999	38	4
$40,000–49,999	17	2
$50,000 and Over	13	1
Not Given	166	19
TOTAL	891	100

Mean Income: $17,490

Table 6.17). About three quarters of the households had only one or two members, and more than 85 percent had no children. The average number of children per household was 0.214, as compared with 0.346 for condominium households. Although about one quarter of the households had more than two occupants, less than 14 percent had children, as compared with 18 percent among condominium households. In fact, children comprised only 10.4 percent of the people in the sample households that lived in rent controlled apartments.

About 27 percent of the households in the sample were married households, over 40 percent fewer than among condominium owners. Of the married households, over 90 percent were over the age of thirty. A small portion—5 percent—of the sample was comprised of single parent households (see Table 6.18). This means that about two thirds of the households in the sample—as compared with about half of the condominium households—were not families in the usual sense of the term—that is they lacked two spouses, lacked children, or lacked both.

An examination of the renters' income distribution, given in Table 6.19, reveals that these households were generally in a moderate income group. While more than 23 percent of the current renter house-holds reported incomes above $20,000, almost 60 percent earned less than $20,000 annually. The mean household income was $17,490, as compared with $27,830 for condominium owners. About 19 percent of the households interviewed did not report their income.[1]

The distribution of income by age of respondent was fairly strongly bimodal. The youngest and the oldest respondents had the lowest in-comes (see Table 6.20). A majority of the households in the under-30 age category and most of the households in the 61-and-over age cate-gory reported earnings of less than $20,000 annually. The yearly in-come of households in the 31–60 age group was weighted more to-ward earnings of over $20,000. These findings are in sharp contrast to the income distribution of condominium owners. The overall income distribution of condominium households by age was more uniform, and older households were more likely to have the highest incomes. More than two thirds of the households interviewed depended on sala-ries or wages as their primary sources of income, as shown in Table 6.21. The second most important sources of income were Social Secu-rity and pension income. Almost one eighth of the households, com-posed mostly of elderly persons, derived their income from Social Se-curity and pensions. The "other" category, which accounts for only 6

---

[1] While this rate of nonresponse to the household income question is typical for a survey of this kind, it is large enough to raise a question as to whether the calculated income distribution among owners and renters is seriously biased because of the types of households that did not provide income data. Nonresponse to the household income question among renters was highest among older households: 34 percent in the 51–60 group, 31 percent in the 61–70 group, and 49 percent in the over-70 group. Similarly, the rate of nonresponse was higher for other characteristics closely correlated in our sample with being older, such as being widowed, retired, and a long-term resident. All other factors, including monthly rent, size of household, and occupation, show no significant correlation with nonresponse to the income question. Is there reason to believe that the nonresponse among the 50-and-over age groups came primarily from either high or low income households? Two pieces of indirect evidence suggest that there is not. First, the pattern of nonresponse among condominium owners is similar to that for renters even though the average income level for all condominium owners is about 60 percent higher than for all renters. Among condominium owners, the total nonresponse rate was 22 percent; the nonresponse rate for the 51–60 age group was 33 percent, for the 61–70 age group 47 percent, and for the over-70 age group 21 percent. Second, the nonresponse rate has no correlation at all with monthly rent, even though rent does bear a relationship to income in our sample. It does not appear, therefore, that the pattern of nonresponses to the household income question significantly biases analyses of other sample characteristics when they are examined in relation to income.

Table 6.20   Income of Renter in Controlled Unit in Relation to Renter's Age

Household Income	Age		
	30 & Under	*31–60*	*61+*
Under $10,000	27%	15%	53%
$10,000–19,999	46	44	35
$20,000–39,999	24	35	7
$40,000 and Over	3	6	5
Total Percentage in Each Age Group	100%	100%	100%
Number (N) of Respondents in Each Age Group	(N=380)	(N=234)	(N=113)
Income Not Given: 164			
Total Respondents: 891			

Table 6.21   Primary Income Source of Renter in Controlled Unit

Primary Income Source	% of Households
Salary/Wages	68
Interest/Dividends	2
Self-Employed	5
Social Security/Pension	12
Other	6
Not Given	7
TOTAL	100
	(N=891)

percent of the households, represents financial support from sources such as parents and scholarships.

Renters were somewhat less likely to be employed than condominium owners (see Table 6.22). Less than 70 percent of the renters were employed, as compared with over 80 percent of the condominium owners. Some of this difference is accounted for by the somewhat larger percentage of households over 65 in the renter group. More than 16 percent of the renters were retired and almost 13 percent were unemployed. The relatively high proportion of respondents who were not in the labor force was also in part due to the large number of women (66 percent) and young persons (46 percent) in the sample, many of whom were college students. Female respondents exhibited a significantly lower rate of labor force participation than male respondents. Women comprised approximately 75 percent of those not in the labor force.

Table 6.22   Occupation of Renter in Controlled Unit by Sex of Respondent

Occupational Status	% of Males	% of Females	% of Males & Females
Employed	(78)	(64)	(69)
Professional	41	39	39
Technical	8	3	5
Managerial	12	7	9
Sales	7	3	4
Clerical	5	11	9
Other°	5	1	2
Do Not Know	2	0	1
Not in Labor Force	(21)	(36)	(31)
Retired	7	21	17
Unemployed	13	15	14
Do Not Know	1	1	1
Total Percentage by Sex	100	100	100
Number (N) of Respondents by Sex	(N=304)	(N=587)	(N=891)

Note: Percentages may not total 100 due to rounding.
° "Other" includes craftsmen, equipment operators, transportation workers, laborers, farm workers, and service and household workers.

A little over half of the males and 46 percent of the females held professional or managerial jobs; both rates were significantly lower than among condominium owners. Females in clerical jobs comprised the next largest occupational group. Males were more heavily represented in the technical, managerial, sales, and "other" occupational categories, and females were more heavily represented in the clerical ranks.

In about 42 percent of the renter households, there was more than one principal job holder, about the same as among condominium owners. Among spouses or other principal household members, the employment rate was the same overall, as shown in Table 6.23, but a larger portion of males than females were unemployed. The overall distribution of jobs held was similar to that of the respondents, but females rather than males had the larger portion of professional or managerial jobs. In general, the pattern of occupational similarity between the two groups of job holders, accompanied by sex differences, closely parallels the pattern among condominium owners.

In summary, members of our sample of current renters in Brookline's controlled units were predominantly single, young, living in one-

Table 6.23 Occupation by Sex of Spouse or Other Principal Condominium Household Member

Occupational Status	% of Males	% of Females	% of Males & Females
Employed	(64)	(72)	(69)
Professional	40	47	44
Technical	6	4	4
Managerial	3	4	4
Sales	5	8	6
Clerical	7	5	6
Other°	4	3	3
Do Not Know	1	2	1
Not in Labor Force	(31)	(24)	(27)
Retired	8	11	10
Unemployed	22	13	17
Do Not Know	5	3	4
Total Percentage by Sex	100	100	100
Number (N) of Responses by Sex	(N=218)	(N=317)	(N=535)

Note: Percentages may not total 100 due to rounding.
° "Other" includes craftsmen, equipment operators, transportation workers, laborers, farm workers, and service and household workers.

or two-member households, and childless, and had annual incomes of less than $20,000. Younger and childless households formed a larger portion of the renter group than in Brookline's condominium owner population. The renters held mainly professional and managerial jobs, though they were less likely to hold such jobs than condominium owners. They also had a somewhat lower labor force participation rate than condominium owners.

Residency Characteristics

Tenants in Brookline's rent controlled units are generally of two types: short-time, high turnover "transients" or long-term "permanent renters" (see Figure 6.1). On the one hand, 45 percent of the sample had resided in Brookline for more than five years and almost one third for more than ten years. On the other hand, a secondary concentration of about one third of the renters in rent controlled units had lived in Brookline less than two years. Most of the respondents under thirty years of age and a majority of those under forty years of age were short-term residents in Brookline (see Table 6.24). In contrast, more

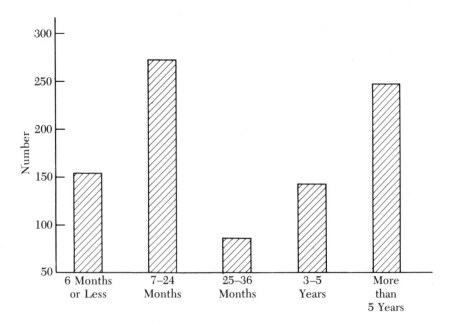

Figure 6.1   Length of Occupancy in Apartment of Renters in Controlled Units.

than 90 percent of the respondents over fifty years of age and more than two thirds of those over forty years of age had resided in Brookline for more than five years.[2]

This bimodal pattern was even more pronounced for length of occupancy in the current apartment. Almost half the renters (47 percent) had lived in their current apartment less than two years, including most (69 percent) of the respondents under thirty years of age. On the other hand, more than 70 percent of the respondents over 40 years of age had lived in their current apartment longer than three years. This more stable residency pattern of older residents was even more marked among households with members over sixty years of age. More than three quarters of these elderly persons had occupied their current apartments for more than five years, which suggests a principal reason condominium conversion is particularly difficult for the elderly.

---

[2] The questionnaire asked only about the length of residency or occupancy of the respondent. In households containing several unrelated persons there may be some difference in the turnover rate (the length of occupancy) as between the respondent and the household as a whole. For instance, while the respondent may have lived in the unit one year, another member of the household may have held a lease on that unit for a longer period. Efforts were made to minimize this difficulty by the interviewer's asking to talk to the head of the household.

Table 6.24 Length of Residence and Occupancy of Renter in Controlled Unit by Age of Respondent

	Age							Total by Length of Residency/Occupancy (%/No.)
Length of Residence in Brookline	30 & Under	31–40	41–50	51–60	61–70	71+	Not Given	
Less than 1 Year	22%	6%	4%	2%	1%	—	7%	12% (107)
1–2 Years	36	18	4	4	1	1	7	21 (188)
2–5 Years	28	30	23	5	3	6	14	22 (194)
5–10 Years	10	24	18	14	9	5	21	13 (114)
10 Years or More	4	22	51	77	86	88	51	32 (287)
Total Percentage in Age Group	100%	100%	100%	100%	100%	100%	100%	100%
Number (N) of Respondents in Each Age Group	(N=413)	(N=177)	(N=56)	(N=44)	(N=93)	(N=93)	(N=14)	(N=890)
Length of Occupancy in Apartment								
6 Months or Less	28%	13%	7%	2%	3%	3%	14%	17% (150)
7–24 Months	41	32	16	14	8	12	28	30 (265)
25–36 Months	13	11	4	7	2	0	7	9 (81)
3–5 Years	14	26	30	18	11	9	0	16 (147)
More than 5 Years	4	18	43	59	76	76	51	28 (246)
Total Percentage in Age Group	100%	100%	100%	100%	100%	100%	100%	100%
Number (N) of Respondents in Each Age Group	(N=413)	(N=177)	(N=56)	(N=44)	(N=93)	(N=93)	(N=14)	(N=891)

Length of residence in Brookline, in contrast to the age of occupant, did not vary uniformly with household income. For example, a significant portion of those earning less than $10,000 annually were short-term residents (under two years), primarily younger people. But, as shown in Table 6.25, there was an almost equally large concentration of persons earning less than $10,000 annually who had resided in Brookline for more than ten years, primarily comprised of older people. A similar bimodal pattern is evident in comparing length of occupancy in the current apartment with income. For example, while almost 40 percent of those earning less than $10,000 annually had occupied their current apartments for less than a year (again, mostly younger people), a nearly equal number had occupied their apartments for more than three years (mostly older people). Among households earning more than $40,000 annually, however, there were almost twice as many long-term versus short-term Brookline residents (46 percent versus 26 percent) and nearly twice as many long-term versus short-term apartment occupants (51 percent versus 26 percent).

These income/age-length of residence/occupancy patterns of correlation are also evident when residence and occupancy are compared with monthly rental levels (see Table 6.26). More than 60 percent of the households surveyed were in the $200–$399 monthly gross rent category. (The weighted average monthly gross rent of the entire sample is $345). Almost half the households that paid monthly gross rents of less than $300 had resided in Brookline for more than five years, and almost 40 percent of the households that paid monthly gross rents of less than $200 had lived in Brookline for more than ten years. In contrast, half of the households that paid monthly gross rents in excess of $500 had lived in Brookline for less than two years.

This pattern is even more pronounced in relation to length of apartment occupancy. For example, approximately half of the households that paid monthly gross rents of less than $300 had occupied their current apartments for more than three years. In contrast, 60 percent of the households that paid monthly gross rents in excess of $500 had occupied their current apartment less than two years.

Rent/Income Relationships

Later in this chapter an analysis of the affordability of condominiums for current renters is presented. Understanding how rent levels corre-

Table 6.25   Length of Residence and Occupancy of Renter in Controlled Unit by Household Income

Length of Residence in Brookline	Income					Total by Length of Residency/Occupancy (%/No.)
	Under $10,000	$10,000–19,999	$20,000–39,999	$40,000 & Over	Not Given	
Less than 1 Year	18%	11%	12%	16%	8%	12% (107)
1–2 Years	20	23	27	10	13	21 (188)
2–5 Years	20	26	26	28	10	22 (194)
5–10 Years	9	14	15	23	12	13 (114)
10 Years or More	33	26	20	23	57	32 (287)
Not Given	—	—	—	—	—	— (1)
Total Percentage by Income Group	100%	100%	100%	100%	100%	100%
Number (N) of Households in Each Income Group	(N=197)	(N=319)	(N=179)	(N=30)	(N=163)	(N=891)
Length of Occupancy in Apartment						
6 Months or Less	22%	16%	20%	13%	11%	17% (150)
7–24 Months	33	32	31	26	19	30 (265)
25–36 Months	7	11	10	10	6	9 (81)
3–5 Years	12	16	23	20	15	16 (147)
More than 5 Years	26	25	16	31	49	28 (246)
Not Given	—	—	—	—	—	— (2)
Total Percentage by Income Group	100%	100%	100%	100%	100%	100%
Number (N) of Households in Each Income Group	(N=197)	(N=319)	(N=179)	(N=30)	(N=163)	(N=891)

Table 6.26 Length of Residence and Occupancy of Renter in Controlled Unit by Monthly Gross Rent

	Monthly Rent						Total by Length of Residency/Occupancy (%/No.)
Length of Residence in Brookline	Less than $200	$200–299	$300–399	$400–500	Over $500	Not Given	
Less than 1 Year	11%	11%	12%	10%	27%	6%	12% (107)
1–2 Years	19	20	23	23	23	6	21 (188)
2–5 Years	22	20	21	29	23	6	22 (194)
5–10 Years	9	13	16	13	7	6	13 (114)
10 Years or More	39	36	28	24	20	76	32 (287)
Not Given	—	—	—	—	—	—	— (1)
Total Percentage by Rent Group	100%	100%	100%	100%	100%	100%	100%
Number (N) of Households in Each Rent Group	(N=54)	(N=240)	(N=304)	(N=168)	(N=74)	(N=50)	(N=891)
Length of Occupancy in Apartment							
6 Months or Less	15%	13%	16%	18%	38%	8%	17% (150)
7–24 Months	23	29	34	33	26	14	30 (265)
25–36 Months	6	10	10	11	7	4	9 (81)
3–5 Years	19	18	14	19	14	14	16 (147)
More than 5 Years	35	30	26	19	15	60	28 (246)
Not Given	2	—	—	—	—	—	— (2)
Total Percentage by Rent Group	100%	100%	100%	100%	100%	100%	100%
Number (N) of Households in Each Rent Group	(N=54)	(N=240)	(N=304)	(N=168)	(N=74)	(N=50)	(N=891)

late with various occupancy characteristics provides useful background for that analysis.

About 70 percent of the units surveyed were one- or two-bedroom units, as shown in Tables 6.27 and 6.28. (This compares with about 80 percent of all rent controlled units in Brookline. See Appendix C.) There was a tendency for younger people to live in larger apartments, and there is a strong correlation between apartment size and monthly rent. This correlation is somewhat blurred, however, when age and monthly rent are compared (see Table 6.29). Thus, because of the small range of predominant apartment types and the strong correlation between apartment size and level of rent, strong age/rent correlations among the Brookline renters in this sample are not evident.

On the other hand, the correlation between income and rent is quite strong, as shown in Table 6.30 and in further detail in Table 6.31. Units with rents under $300 per month generally were occupied by households earning less than $20,000 annually. In contrast, units with rents in excess of $500 monthly were occupied mostly by households earning more than $20,000 annually. The proportion of income spent on rent declined as income increased, as Table 6.31 shows.

Summary. Rental households in the controlled units in Brookline were predominantly under thirty years of age, were concentrated in one- and two-bedroom units, and typically paid rents in the $200–$399 category. The $200–$399 rent level was typical of households that had average household incomes of less than $20,000 annually. Generally, these households, which were usually childless and comprised of two persons, had resided in Brookline and had occupied their current apartments for less than two years.

A majority of the elderly households were one-person households. These persons were typically longer-term residents who had lived in Brookline for more than ten years and had occupied their one- or two-bedroom apartments for more than five years. These apartments typically rented in the $200–$399 category, a category appropriate to these households' incomes of less than $20,000 annually.

The middle aged renters were longer-term Brookline residents and had occupied their one- or two-bedroom apartments for a longer period of time than the younger households but not as long as the elderly households. The middle-aged renters also lived in units that typically rented in the $200–$399 category, but they paid a lower average monthly rent than the younger households even though they had a somewhat higher annual income.

Table 6.27 Number of Bedrooms in Rent Controlled Units by Age of Respondent

No. of Bedrooms	Age							Total of Each Unit Size (%/No.)
	30 & Under	31–40	41–50	51–60	61–70	71 +	Not Given	
0	4%	3%	2%	9%	8%	5%	7%	4% (38)
1	28	36	32	20	49	43	30	33 (296)
2	37	36	35	43	35	46	21	37 (333)
3	19	20	16	23	4	4	21	16 (145)
4 or More	9	5	13	5	4	0	0	9 (72)
Not Given	3	0	2	0	0	2	21	1 (7)
Total Percentage by Age Group	100%	100%	100%	100%	100%	100%	100%	100%
Number (N) of Respondents in Each Age Group	(N=413)	(N=177)	(N=56)	(N=44)	(N=93)	(N=93)	(N=14)	(N=891)

Table 6.28 Gross Monthly Rent Paid by Renters in Controlled Units by Number of Bedrooms in Unit

No. of Bedrooms	Monthly Rent						Total of Households in Each Income Group (%/No.)
	Less than $200	$200–299	$300–399	$400–500	Over 500	Rent Not Given	
0	24%	7%	1%	1%	—	6%	44% (38)
1	57	51	33	12	4	36	33 (296)
2	7	31	49	43	23	36	37 (333)
3	6	8	15	30	27	12	16 (145)
4 or More	4	3	2	13	45	2	9 (72)
Not Given	2	0	0	1	1	8	1 (7)
Total Percentage by Rent Group	100%	100%	100%	100%	100%	100%	100%
Number (N) of Households in Each Rent Group	(N=54)	(N=240)	(N=304)	(N=168)	(N=74)	(N=50)	(N=891)

Table 6.29 Monthly Gross Rent Paid by Renters in Controlled Units by Age of Respondent

Monthly Gross Rent	Age							Total Respondents in Each Rent Group (%/No.)
	30 & Under	31-40	41-50	51-60	61-70	71+	Not Given	
Less Than $200	5%	6%	2%	9%	8%	9%	14%	6% (54)
$200-299	26	29	41	20	31	10	14	27 (240)
$300-399	36	41	27	41	27	27	7	34 (304)
$400-500	20	17	16	23	15	22	7	19 (168)
Over $500	11	5	9	7	6	4	7	8 (74)
Not Given	2	2	5	0	13	19	51	6 (50)
Total Percentage by Age Group	100%	100%	100%	100%	100%	100%	100%	100%
Number (N) of Respondents in Each Age Group	(N=413)	(N=177)	(N=56)	(N=14)	(N=93)	(N=93)	(N=14)	(N=890)

Table 6.30 Monthly Gross Rent Paid by Renters in Controlled Units by Household Income

Household Income	Monthly Rent						Total of Households in Each Income Group (%/No.)
	Less Than $200	*$200–299*	*$300–399*	*$400–500*	*Over 500*	*Not Given*	
Under $10,000	42%	33%	16%	16%	14%	20%	22% (197)
$10,000–19,999	35	46	40	30	19	14	36 (319)
$20,000–39,999	4	10	26	32	26	2	20 (179)
$40,000 and Over	0	0	2	4	20	2	3 (30)
Not Given	19	11	16	18	21	62	18 (163)
Total Percentage by Rent Group	100%	100%	100%	100%	100%	100%	99%
Number (N) of Households in Each Rent Group	(N=54)	(N=240)	(N=304)	(N=168)	(N=74)	(N=50)	(N=888)

Table 6.31   Annual Income of Renters in Controlled Units by Monthly Gross Rent

No. of Households	Household Income	Average Monthly Gross Rent	Rent as % of Income
186	Less than $10,000	$280	45°
312	$10,000–19,999	$330	26
140	$20,000–29,999	$375	18
38	$30,000–39,999	$425	15
17	$40,000–49,999	$455	12
12	$50,000–Over	$500+	—
705			

Mean Income: $17,490
Mean Rent: $345
Mean Rent/Income Ratio: 28%

° Assumes an average income of $7,500.

Principal, Secondary, and Tertiary Household Profiles

The characteristics described above can be summarized in profile groups analogous to those established for condominium purchasers.

A. *Principal Household Profile*

1. Young household, median age of head under thirty years; generally not married.
2. Mean size 2.32 persons; generally have not yet entered family-rearing stage of life.
3. Average household income $17,072 per year.
4. Principal source of income salary or wages; other sources, such as parental support, reflect student status of many respondents.
5. Length of residence in current unit generally two years or less.
6. Units typically one- or two-bedroom apartments with monthly gross rent in $200–$399 range.

B. *Secondary Household Profile*

1. Elderly household, median age of head in sixties; generally no longer married or, frequently, never married.
2. Households relatively small, mean size 1.49 persons; may be termed "empty nesters"—in post-child rearing stage of life.
3. Households of moderate means, average income $13,827 per year.

4. Principal source of income Social Security or pensions.
5. Length of residence in current unit generally exceeds five years.
6. Units almost all one- or two-bedroom apartments with gross rents broadly dispersed across $200–$500 range.

C. Tertiary Household Profile

1. Middle-aged household not in process of family rearing, head generally between thirty-one and forty years of age; generally not married.
2. Mean size 2.12 persons.
3. Most affluent of renter households, with median income tending toward $20,000.
4. Principal source of income professional or managerial job.
5. Longer term residents, majority having lived in current unit more than three years.
6. Units typically one- or two-bedrooms, generally renting in vicinity of $350 monthly.

In sum, renters in Brookline were largely single, whether they were young multiperson or single person households or older "empty nesters." They were also generally in the lower income brackets either because they were just starting their careers or because their working lives were behind them. Even the middle aged households tended to be in the moderate income range and most often were neither married nor had children. Brookline renters were fairly transient if they were younger and quite stable if middle aged or older.

Characteristics of Renters Displaced by Conversion

The sample of displaced tenants we were able to interview is small— only 22. While a good deal of useful information about the impact of the conversion process on this group was gained from these interviews, the sample is too small to support valid extrapolations to all such households. The analyses of these interviews are therefore more qualitative and less quantitative than those of the renters and the condominium owners.

The small sample size is primarily a function of the difficulty of identifying and tracing people who had moved from their former residences. An initial list of 75 names, obtained with the help of tenant

Table 6.32   Comparison of Renters in Controlled Units and Displaced Tenants

	Renters	*Displaced Tenants*
Age		
Under 30	47%	32%
31–60	31%	27%
Over 60	20%	27%
NA	2%	14%
Mean Income	$17,490	$21,316
Married	27%	28%
Children as Percentage of All Household		
Members	10%	2%
Average Household Size	2.05	1.91
Length of Occupancy		
Less than 2 Years	47%	32%
2–5 Years	25%	27%
Over 5 Years	28%	41%
Occupation		
Professional or Managerial	48%	67%
Retired	16%	14%
Average Rent (pre-conversion)	$345	$382
Average Rent/Income Ratio (pre-conversion)	24%	22%

groups, shrank because of addresses that were not adequate for tracing, moves subsequent to initial moves, and other incomplete information. The final sample includes people who had moved some considerable distance from Brookline, such as to Cape Cod or Florida.

Comparisons between the displaced tenants and the larger group of current renters of which they were a part reveal no substantial differences. In comparison to current renters (see Table 6.32), the displaced tenants tended to be a little older and tended to have somewhat higher incomes. The occupational mix was not drastically different, with two thirds of the displaced tenants having professional or managerial jobs, as opposed to half of the current renters. About the same small proportion was retired and living on Social Security or pensions.

Household size was somewhat smaller among the displaced tenants, partly because they had so few children (only 1, or 2 percent, compared with about 10 percent for the renter group) and partly because there were fewer multi-member single person households.

The displaced tenants' tenure in the Brookline apartments that were converted tended to be somewhat longer than for renters. There was, in fact, a fairly large portion of long-term (over five years) tenants, which is probably one of the reasons for this group's strongly negative reactions to having to relocate.

The 22 percent of income the displaced tenants spent on housing in the pre-conversion apartments was fairly low, which perhaps suggests why the added cost of a condominium seemed out of reach for many of them.

It is often asserted that the relocation caused by the conversion process has a particularly harsh effect on the poor and the elderly. This statement may be interpreted either as meaning that a disproportionate number of poor or elderly end up moving as a result of conversion or that forced relocation is more difficult for the poor and the elderly to cope with. While the second interpretation is almost certainly true, our data do not support the first interpretation. The displaced tenants we reached for interviews were neither the poorest nor the oldest people in the total renter population.

Changes Resulting from Conversion

The changes being wrought in Brookline's population as a result of condominium conversion can be brought into focus from two perspectives. First, by comparing the household characteristics of renters, condominium owners, and displaced tenants; and second, by understanding what the economic consequences would be for renters who purchased their apartments if they were converted.

Trends in Household Characteristics

The sets of profile groups provide a useful way to summarize the changes that are taking place in household characteristics as a result of conversion. As condominium owners replace renters, the 30-and-under age group becomes a smaller portion of the population. Among renters, this group is the principal profile group, but among owners it is the secondary group. Although the under-30 owner households are more likely to be married and to have children, the average household size decreases as owners replace renters—2.32 to 1.86, a decrease of 20 percent. This is mainly because the under-30 renter households are far more likely to include more than two adults than are owner households. As owners replace renters, the average annual income for this age group increases from $17,072 to $24,961, an increase of 46 percent. Wage earners in condominium owner households are also more likely to hold managerial or professional jobs.

The 31–60 age group, the tertiary group among renters, becomes the principal group among owners. These owner households are more likely to be married than are renters of the same age group, but the owners are still not very likely to have children. Their household size is only slightly smaller than that of the renter group. The median income increases from about $20,000 to about $28,000, an increase of over 40 percent. Both renters and owners in this age group are likely to be longer-term (over three years) residents of Brookline.

The 61-or-older age group, the secondary group among renters, becomes the tertiary group among owners. The owners in this group are somewhat more likely to be married and tend on average to be a little more likely to live in two-person households. The household size increases from 1.49 for renters to 1.60 for owners. The income differential between owners and renters is the largest among the three groups. Average income increases from $13,827 to $28,449, an increase of 106 percent. The primary reason for this increase is the far greater likelihood of interest or dividends being the primary income sources for these older households instead of Social Security or pensions. Both renters and owners 61 or older tend to be longer-term residents of Brookline.

Because half of the condominium owners in our sample previously lived in Brookline, it appears that conversion is encouraging the residency of certain types of households already well represented in Brookline and at the same time is discouraging other types of resident groups from staying. Many of the new condominium owners, far from being newcomers, had lived in Brookline a long time. Moreover, many of the new condominium owners moving to Brookline are quite similar in age, income, occupation, and other characteristics to these older residents. But whatever their origins, as these new condominium owners become a larger proportion of Brookline's population, they will displace renters of quite different types. If conversion continues, Brookline's population, on the evidence of our sample data, will become significantly more affluent, more married, somewhat older, and less transient.

Housing Cost Implications of Conversion for Renters

The average monthly carrying costs of a condominium are significantly higher than the cost of a comparable apartment, even though tax deductions are available that lower net carrying costs. How many current renter households would be able to afford these higher costs if their apartments were converted to condominiums? The following analysis addresses this question and the implications of its answers.

Cash Flow Implications. The average rent of the current renters in our sample was $345 monthly. Based on data described in Chapter 3, the average condominium sells for 118 times its former monthly rent. Thus a unit renting for $345 monthly would cost $41,700 (118 × $345) and would have average gross monthly carrying costs of $590. The average income tax deductions for mortgage interest and property tax payments on this average unit are approximately $92 and $109, respectively, for married couples filing jointly and single heads of households. Accordingly, the net monthly carrying costs of newly converted units currently renting at the $345 average monthly rent would be about $481 and $498, respectively, for these two household types. (The methodology for arriving at these figures is described in Appendix D.)

Table 6.33 displays the relationship between household income ranges and estimates of after tax carrying charges for apartments after conversion to condominiums. The pre-conversion rent is the average rent for each income group based on the sample data.

For households with annual incomes in excess of $20,000, the estimated post-conversion carrying costs are in a range that is comparable to the rents currently paid as a percent of income. However, the average annual income of all households in the renter sample was less than $20,000; in fact, 71 percent of the households had incomes of less than $20,000. For renters with less than $10,000 of annual household income, the figures in Table 6.33 show a very substantial mismatch between renters' current resources and the net post-conversion carrying costs of the units they currently rent. Monthly carrying costs could consume as much as 81–83 percent of the income of these households. The figures also indicate that renters who have between $10,000 and $20,000 of annual household income and who would, in theory, be able to purchase the converted units, might have to devote as much as 38–39 percent of their incomes to shelter if they did so.

Table 6.33   Household Incomes of Renters in Controlled Units in Relation to Cost of Units as Condominiums

Household Income	Number of Households	% of Total	Current Average Gross Monthly Rent		Estimated Average After-Tax Monthly Cost of Apartment as a Condominium	
			Rent	% of Income	Cost	% of Income
Under $10,000	186	26	$280	45	$506–520	81–83
$10,000–19,999	312	45	$330	26	$479–494	38–39
$20,000–29,999	140	20	$375	18	$478–501	23–24
$30,000–39,999	38	5	$425	15	$474–504	16–17
$40,000–49,999	17	2	$455	12	$455–485	12–13
$50,000+	12	2	$500+	—	—	—

Total Households: 705

Mean Income: $17,490
Mean Gross Monthly Rent: $345, or 24% of monthly income
Mean Monthly Carrying Cost: from $481 (33%) of income to $498 (34%) of income

Note: See Appendix D for explanation of calculations.

Table 6.34 Cash Flow Implications of Condominium Conversion for Renters in Controlled Units

Household Type	Average Income	Gross Monthly Rent	Rent/Income Ratio
Type 1 (30 and Under)	$17,072	$358	0.25
Type 2 (61 and Over)	$13,827	$335	0.29
Type 3 (31–60)	$19,989	$338	0.20

Household Type	Projected Condominium Offering Price	Monthly Condominium Cost (MCC)	MCC/ Income Ratio	Percent Increase in Housing Cost
Type 1 (30 and Under)	$41,528	$495–512	0.35–0.36	38–43%
Type 2 (61 and Over)	$39,530	$466–483	0.40–0.42	39–44%
Type 3 (31–60)	$39,884	$492–506	0.30	46–50%

To show more clearly the cost implications of condominium conversion which face current renters in Brookline's controlled units, we have reformulated the analysis presented above in terms of the three renter household types described earlier. Table 6.34 shows the results of this analysis by displaying median incomes, average rents, and rent/income ratios for the three renter household types. A projected average condominium offering price, computed by applying the appropriate factor to the average monthly rent, is also included for each of the three household types. The results are shown in the higher cost/income ratios and in the percentage increases in shelter costs which would result for each of the major household types if their present apartments were converted to condominiums.

While current renters in Brookline generally appear to reside in housing units whose costs are reasonably matched to their incomes, the condominium conversion process threatens a change in this relationship of serious proportions. The cost consequences of converting apartments to condominiums would likely make these dwelling units unavailable to most of the households described in the secondary renter profile. The households in the principal profile might be able to purchase the converted units by devoting approximately one third of their income to shelter costs.

If conversion continues in Brookline at a substantial pace, what is the likelihood that as many as 50–70 percent of current renters will be forced to choose between significantly increasing the proportion of income they spend on housing or moving? Any intelligent response to this question must take into account the substantial turnover rate of current renters. As noted above, almost half of all renters move within two years. Most of these transients are relatively young lower income people. Condominium purchase is generally not a strong interest for most of this group. (See Chapter 2 for data to support this view.) If their apartments were converted, the hardship they would face as a group would probably not be severe, since they might well be moving in the near future anyway. The principal result of conversion would be (as noted above) that this group would be replaced by older, more affluent condominium owners. But for longer-term residents, many of whom are older people, the situation is quite different. They are not only frequently unable to afford the higher condominium costs but have a strong desire not to move.

Even after identifying these two groups, with their very different tenancy characteristics, the proportion of Brookline's current renter population which may be faced with actual buy-or-move choices cannot be estimated with any assurance. What is indisputable, however, based on the comparative cost analysis presented above, is that for the less transient, less affluent, and generally older groups in Brookline, conversion of their apartments will generally have the effect of putting the apartments in a price range they cannot afford.

Continued conversion, in other words, will inevitably lead to a significant upward movement in the average income level of Brookline's residents as current renters are displaced by condominium owners. This observation is confirmed not only by the cost effects of owning versus renting just analyzed but also by the differences between the three renter and three owner profile groups.

Investment Implications. The foregoing cost comparisons have been made in terms of the estimated annual cash flow of potential condominium owners—that is, we have estimated the basic out-of-pocket expenses for housing and have adjusted them by applying the tax reductions that can be achieved by deducting real estate taxes and mortgage interest payments. This approach, however, neglects significant capital or investment considerations.

One of the principal reasons given for condominium ownership, as described in Chapter 2, is the opportunity to accumulate the capital that is represented by an owner's equity in a condominium. Equity builds up through monthly mortgage payments, and more significantly in the last few years in Brookline, through the inflation in condominium prices. While rent control in Brookline has protected renters from some of the inflation in housing costs, residents are generally aware of how much housing costs have escalated. The desire to achieve some protection against housing cost inflation, as well as the opportunity to realize a gain from an investment, are significant factors in leading many people to buy condominiums.

By the same token, the increase in the value of the investment in the condominium represents an increase in wealth for the owner. When someone is considering purchasing a condominium, this potential increase in equity can be as significant an economic consideration as the out-of-pocket cost calculation. A complete analysis of condominium/rental economics would take this equity accumulation into account. Counterbalancing the equity considerations is the potential loss in income caused by investing a down payment in a condominium. If, for example, a $10,000 down payment were assembled by withdrawing that sum from a savings account, the loss of interest—say, at 8 percent, or more than $800 per year—would have to be counted as a cost of ownership.

These investment/savings considerations are real in economic terms. They offer both actual and potential economic advantages for condominium ownership in comparison to paying rent. But they are advantages that make sense only to people who, for whatever reason, want to purchase a condominium. For an elderly couple, for instance, living on a fixed income and from assets accumulated in their earning years, the prospect of putting some of their available cash into a condominium as an investment for the future would probably be unappealing. For this reason and because the calculation of capital costs and returns is subject to many arbitrary assumptions, we have not estimated the economic value of these additional economic considerations. While this omission may leave our analysis open to the charge of incompleteness, we believe the earlier cash flow calculations represent the condominium purchase issue as it is viewed by renters who are mainly concerned with the out-of-pocket housing costs of owning a condominium.

Chapter 7

PROJECTED EFFECTS OF CONTINUED CONVERSION ON BROOKLINE'S FISCAL CONDITION

The conversion of rental apartments to condominiums affects a community's property tax rate in two principal ways. The primary impact on a community comes from the revaluation of converted property: the tax on a building is higher when all of its units are assessed as condominiums than when the building as a whole is assessed as a rental property. The community experiences a secondary and smaller impact through changes in the demands for municipal services caused by the arrival of condominium households whose characteristics are different from those of departing renter households.

In order to estimate the future fiscal effects of conversion, we have followed a three-step process. The first step is to compare the pattern of property tax assessments on condominiums to the pattern for rental buildings, based on the experience of the last few years in Brookline. The second step is to develop a series of alternative assumptions about the rate at which buildings may be converted in Brookline over the next five years. A great many factors influence the rate of condominium conversion, most of which are subject to unpredictable changes. Therefore, the assumptions used are only reasonable hypotheses; they are not predictions of what is likely to occur in Brookline. The final step is to calculate the increases in property taxes which would result under these alternative assumptions. These increases are then modi-

117

fied upward or downward to reflect the changes in demand for municipal services that may be caused by the changing household characteristics associated with conversions.

The result of this three-step process will be to permit us to answer
some "what if" questions. What if, for instance, conversions continue
at the recent rate for the next five years? How many units would be
converted, and what would be the tax impacts? Answers to hypothetical questions like this do not, of course, represent predictions about
what will happen. But they do provide a good idea of what the future
might look like if certain types of events took place.

Comparison of Tax Valuation Methods for Condominiums and Rental Properties

For purposes of real estate tax assessments, income-producing and
non-income-producing properties are generally valued in different
ways. Income-producing property, whether it is rental housing or a
commercial property like a store, is valued in Brookline and in many
other places in relation to the stream of income produced. The basic
logic of this approach is that since the owner's purpose in holding the
property is generally to produce an income from rents or leases, the
property has value only in relation to how much income it actually
produces. Two parcels of the same type of property—for instance,
two identical McDonald's outlets—will generally be valued differently for tax purposes if one of them produces a significantly larger
sales volume than the other, all other factors being equal. Similarly,
two one-bedroom apartments, similar in size, layout, and general condition, will probably be valued differently if one commands a significantly higher rent than the other, perhaps because it is in a better
location. By the same token, if rents rise in a building, the building's
valuation generally will also increase. For example, whenever the
Brookline Rent Control Board has granted a special or general rent
increase, the assessed valuations of the apartment buildings affected
generally have increased. There are other ways of valuing income
property, including rental housing, but since this is the method used in
Brookline it has been used as the basis for the tax impacts estimated in
this study.

Non-income property is commonly valued in Brookline and elsewhere in relation to its market value—that is, it is valued in relation to

the price it would bring on the open market if sold. One way to determine a condominium unit's market value is to look at the sales prices paid for comparable units. When a building is converted from income or rental status to non-income or condominium status, an additional set of factors affect its tax valuation. The developer must invest some capital to convert the units. As noted above, this includes "hard costs," the costs of physical improvements or rehabilitation, and "soft costs," costs such as rental loss, marketing expenses, and legal fees. Developers, of course, expect to recover all of these costs and in addition expect to earn a profit through the price they can get for the units on the market. The new tax valuation is based on this market value—that is, the valuation includes the improvements and conversion costs added during the conversion process as well as the developer's profits, to the extent that these costs are recovered in the sales price. The higher tax assessment of converted units is partly a reflection of these additions to cost and the profit.

The market price—and therefore the tax valuation—of a condominium is related to its valuation as a rental unit in a more fundamental way. The price of a converted condominium is related fairly directly to the rental cost of the unit when it was an apartment. As noted in Chapter 3, this relationship—the sales price/rent ratio—varies in Brookline within a fairly narrow range and averaged about 118 times monthly rent in our sample. In other words, an apartment renting for $345 per month (the average for all rent controlled units in our telephone survey) would sell on average at 118 times this figure, or $40,710. (In fact, the average price calculated from our telephone sample of condominium owners was $37,263.)

Because the tax valuation of a condominium is based on its market price, the valuation, by the above logic, is also related in some manner to the unit's previous assessment as a rental apartment. An examination of a sample of building assessments before and after conversion substantiates this general relationship. For the sample of 21 buildings we analyzed, the post-conversion valuation was on average 34 percent higher than the pre-conversion valuation (see Table 7.1). This difference represents in part the value added to a rental unit in the conversion process. The difference in valuations may also reflect the effect of excess market demand on condominium prices. In other words, a supply shortage may drive a unit's price up more than may be warranted by the improvements added and the costs incurred in the conversion process.

Table 7.1   Post-Conversion Tax Assessment Increases for a Sample* of Brookline Buildings Converted 1977–1979

Building	Pre-Conversion Assessment	Post-Conversion Assessment	Percentage Difference
5–19 Alton Ct. and 31 Alton Pl.	$ 226,000	$ 315,000	39.4
120–126 Amory St.	230,000	287,500	25.0
1–10 Auburn Ct.	270,000	510,000	88.9
1793 Beacon St.	71,000	74,800	5.4
120 Beaconsfield Rd.†	500,000	1,300,000	142.6
22 Chestnut Pl.†	1,050,000	642,900	− 38.8
30 Dean Rd. and 149 Beaconsfield Rd.	115,000	115,000	0
15 Francis St.	370,000	388,500	5.0
202–208 Fuller St.	225,000	225,000	0
11 Garrison Rd.	60,000	98,000	63.3
16 Garrison Rd.	64,000	90,000	40.6
50 Green St.	720,000	970,700	34.8
77–83 Harvard Ave.	150,000	288,000	92.0
41 Park St.	690,000	763,300	10.6
33–39 St. Paul St.	260,000	350,000	34.6
194 St. Paul St.	46,000	46,000	0
311–325 Tappan St. and 222–224 Rawson Rd.	525,000	964,000	83.6
337–343 Tappan St. and 54–56 Garrison Rd.	225,000	316,000	23.9
563–573 Washington St. and 86–94 Griggs Rd.	520,000	604,500	16.3
576 Washington St.	78,000	78,000	0
119–127 Winthrop Rd.	210,000	286,900	36.6
Total	$5,055,000	$6,771,200	34.0%

Source: Harbridge House, Inc., 1979, based on records from Town Assessor's Office.
* For description of sample see page 24.
† Building excluded from totals because recorded data appear to be incorrect.

Another factor affecting post-conversion as compared to pre-conversion valuation is rent control. Because rent control keeps rents at below-market levels, the increase in the tax valuation of a building after it has been converted may well be larger than it would have been in the absence of rent control. Put another way, because one effect of rent control is to reduce the rental income produced by a building to a lower level than it would be without rent control, the building's tax valuation—since it is based on income—will also be lower. When a building is converted, the effects of rent control on the building's assessment are eliminated and the resulting assessment may thus be proportionately higher. The overall average increase of 34 percent in building valuations, therefore, also reflects the history of assessments on rent controlled buildings, including abatements or other considerations reflecting some unique characteristic of a building as a rental property.

In sum, several factors account for the different tax yields of a building before and after conversion. These factors principally include the improvements in and profits on a building resulting from conversion, the effects of strong demand in driving up condominium prices, and the effects of rent control in depressing the assessed valuation of pre-conversion buildings. Because the basis of valuing buildings for tax purposes differs between income-producing and non-income-producing buildings, it is not possible to quantify individually each of the effects of these or other relevant factors on increasing a building's post-conversion assessment. The net effect, however, is to produce the 34 percent increase in post-conversion assessments noted above. The magnitude of this increase is simply an empirical observation based on a fairly large sample of buildings. While it has certain limitations, the 34 percent figure provides a plausible basis for projecting future tax revenue increases generated by condominium conversions.

Because the ratio between pre- and post-conversion tax valuations varies so widely from building to building, a more careful statistical analysis was made of the relationship between pre-conversion rents and post-conversion valuations in order to understand better the tax consequences of conversion. The formula that expresses this relationship, which is shown in Appendix C, roughly produces the following figures. Every dollar of monthly rent (or $12 of annual rent) will result in an average of about $52 of assessed valuation on the converted condominiums. Thus, using the 1979 tax rate of $98 per thousand dollars of assessed valuation, one dollar of pre-conversion monthly rent will average about $5 of post-conversion taxes. Using this formula, an apartment in an average 20-unit building renting for $350 per month will have an average valuation of $17,995 as a condominium. How does this $17,995 compare to the pre-conversion valuation? Based on our analysis of past assessing practices (see Table 7.1), the $350-a-month apartment would typically be valued for tax purposes at $13,429; that is, the post-conversion valuation would be 34 percent higher than the pre-conversion valuation. At 1979 property tax rates in Brookline, this valuation would yield an additional $447.47 in tax revenues.

Factors Affecting Future Rate of Conversion

Having established a procedure for converting current monthly rents into future condominium tax revenues, we next considered the rate at which rental apartments might be converted in future years. The future rate of conversion is subject to so many factors that cannot be estimated with any certainty or precision that it is unproductive to try to predict this rate. Instead, we propose to develop two hypothetical models as a means of illustrating the consequences of using two different assumptions about the conversion rate.

First, it will be useful to consider the factors that are likely to influence the conversion rate. These factors fall into three general categories: supply-related factors, demand-related factors, and regulatory-related factors.

Supply-Related Factors

The supply of buildings suitable for conversion in Brookline is, of course, limited. Of the approximately 900 unconverted rent controlled buildings remaining in late 1979 (containing about 9,000 units), some have physical or locational characteristics that make them more desirable for conversion than others. Buildings in the most convenient locations in relation to public transit, with good unit layouts, with parking, in sound physical condition, and in higher rent ranges are the most desirable for conversion. The less favorable a building's characteristics are, the harder it will be for a developer or landlord to sell units in it. At what point a building is no longer attractive for conversion because its characteristics are too unfavorable is a function of what prospective buyers are willing to settle for in terms of housing amenities and of whether the price buyers are willing to pay for units with fewer amenities will assure the developer his or her expected profit. Some developers have estimated that as much as 75 percent of Brookline's rent controlled buildings could not be converted profitably; others feel the percentage is much lower—perhaps only 25 percent. Either estimate, of course, is to some extent a function of prevailing market conditions.

Building ownership characteristics are also a significant supply factor. Even if a building is physically attractive for conversion, its current landlord may have no interest in selling it. A landlord may, for instance, be interested in the long-term income stream, which under the right debt and depreciation structure can be in good part tax free or sheltered. The profit on a sale would probably be subject to a sizeable capital gains tax. Moreover, some landlords, as noted in Chapter 3, see their buildings as a sort of "living trust" for their children. In some buildings, according to some of our informants, the existing mortgage contains flat prohibitions against prepayment, making conversion impossible until the mortgage term expires.

On the other hand, conversion is seen by many landlords as an attractive "out" from a rent control situation they believe denies them the return on their investments they believe is commensurate with what they could get elsewhere in the real estate market or by using their invested capital in other ways. Many buildings, for instance, have long-standing mortgages. The owner might well want to convert equity in such a building, which is derived from repaid principal and the appreciation or inflation in the building's value, into a liquid form in order to reinvest it elsewhere. Our inquiries reveal that in the current rent control situation almost no bank is willing to refinance a rent controlled building on which it holds a mortgage. Thus, refinancing is usually not a feasible way for a landlord to regain use of his or her invested capital. Many banks, however, are willing to convert an existing mortgage into a condominium mortgage. These bank practices thus create an incentive for some landlords to convert, either by themselves or by selling their buildings to developers.

As a landlord's personal or business circumstances change and as the real estate market changes, perhaps because of tightened credit, his preferences concerning conversion may change from more willing to less willing, or the reverse. It is, of course, extremely difficult to estimate what the current division of sentiments regarding selling or holding is among all of Brookline's landlords and even more difficult to predict how these sentiments may change.

In addition to building condition and landlord preferences, the presence of developers willing and able to convert buildings is a significant supply consideration. As noted in Chapter 3, converting a building successfully—that is, selling all units at a profit—requires considerable knowledge, skill, and willingness to take financial risks. There are perhaps no more than six to eight developers active on any significant scale in Brookline (excluding individual landlords who choose to convert their own buildings)—not a large number. Moreover, most larger developers require access to capital to make conversion possible.

On the other hand, as long as there is a strong demand for condominiums from buyers able to secure unit mortgage money, it seems likely that capable developers will be able to make an acceptable profit from conversions. And this fact is likely to assure that there will always be some developers active in the Brookline market. The rate at which buildings are converted, however, will vary considerably in relation to how potential developers react to changing conditions in the housing market.

Demand-Related Factors

The demand for condominiums in Brookline is fueled by several inter-related forces: the desire of families for financial security and home ownership; the availability of mortgage money; the price of housing in Brookline; and the attractiveness of Brookline as a place to live. The supply of single family houses in Brookline has been essentially static for some time. The average price of a single family home sold in Brookline in 1979 was $104,000 (see Chapter 2). If home ownership in Brookline is a family's goal, therefore, condominiums in the $30,000–60,000 range are quite attractive for families below the upper-income level. The principal reasons cited by condominium owners in our sample for purchasing their units related to price/quality and location considerations (see Chapter 2).

Is it likely that the relative attractiveness of condominiums in Brookline will decrease? Probably not. At $30–40 per square foot, Brookline condominiums are not expensive relative to condominium prices elsewhere in the Boston area. Prices in 1979 in the Back Bay area of Boston, for instance, ranged from $80 per square foot to well over $100. In the neighboring communities of Cambridge and New-ton, in which few condominiums are on the market, prices are comparable to those in Brookline. The basic attractiveness of Brookline as a location and as a community to live in is relatively immune from short-term changes.

On the other hand, the availability of mortgage money may well become the most critical short-run factor. Only 10 percent of the condominium owners in our sample got their mortgage money from a source other than a bank. Developers funded only 2 percent of the mortgages, and in a tight credit situation developers are unlikely to be able to fund mortgages banks are unable to fund.

A credit squeeze producing mortgage interest rates of 13–14 percent or higher was unprecedented prior to 1980. How the local savings banks and savings and loans that provide most of the condominium mortgage funds in Brookline will deal with such a situation is uncertain. Our extensive interviews with these banks reveal, however, that without exception they give preference to single family or even two or three family (owner-occupied) homes over condominiums. This preference is evident, for instance, in the common bank practice of requiring larger down payments for condominiums and of charging 0.25–0.50 percent higher interest rates, either directly or by charging points to the borrower. Thus as credit tightens, condominium mortgages are apt to decline in availability more rapidly than home mortgages.

In this connection, it is relevant to note that as a result of the 1974–1975 recession, during which the real estate market suffered major losses and credit was tight, condominium conversion in Brookline slowed drastically. In 1975 only three buildings containing 15 units were converted and in 1976 only one building with 4 units. These statistics contrast with 71–149 units per year in the preceding four years (see Figure 2.1). Another credit squeeze could have a similar impact on conversions.

A possible mitigating factor in the credit squeeze could be the use of the secondary mortgage market by Brookline banks. Only one or two of the banks that serve the Brookline condominium market have made extensive use of Freddie Mac (Federal Home Loan Mortgage Corporation) or Ginnie Mae (Government National Mortgage Association) as a source of mortgage capital. Many savings and loans in California, for instance, immediately sell their mortgages to one or both of these institutions, thus quickly recycling their capital and making it available for mortgages once again. Because many of the banks serving the Brookline condominium market have made so little use of this secondary market, a change in the policies of these banks towards secondary markets could help mitigate any credit squeeze, assuming that Freddie Mac and Ginnie Mae funds continue to be available.

Having recognized that Brookline condominiums will continue to be attractive and leaving aside for a moment the problems of credit availability, are there enough potential new buyers of the type who are now purchasing condominiums in Brookline? There probably are. About half of all condominium purchasers we surveyed in Brookline had Brookline as their previous residence. Twenty-three percent lived in the same building in which they purchased and another 26 percent lived elsewhere in Brookline, including 19 percent who rented in apartment buildings (see Table 6.9). If the 42 percent ratio of those living in controlled apartments (23 percent who rented in the converted buildings, plus 19 percent who rented elsewhere) holds in the future, this would provide about 3,800 potential buyers for condominiums from those who rent in Brookline's approximately 9,000 remaining controlled units, plus a significant number who own or rent houses in Brookline. If this potential pool of Brookline resident condominium buyers totalled 4,200, this pool would translate into about 8,400 condominium units at the current ratio of about one "outsider" to every one Brookline resident.

This calculation is, of course, a very crude one. It could be argued that a disproportionate share of Brookline residents who are likely to purchase condominiums have already done so, or alternatively, that as condominiums become more widespread in Brookline their popularity will rise. Some evidence that the latter hypothesis is more likely has come from developers who find a decreasing need to advertise condominiums because an ample number of buyers come forth informed only by word of mouth. This occurs particularly with larger, family-size units.

Thus, while our evidence is at best qualitative and inferential, there appears to be little basis to assert that the potential demand for Brookline condominiums is close to being exhausted. If the pace of conversions in Brookline diminishes in the future, it seems unlikely that a lack of interested buyers will be the cause. On the other hand, if mortgage funds are unavailable, potential buyers of condominiums will have to postpone their purchases, with a consequent large fall-off in the rate of conversions.

Regulatory Related Factors

The manner in which Brookline regulates condominium conversion is, of course, a key influence on the rate of conversion. There is not much evidence that the ban on conversion-related evictions imposed in May 1979, is yet significantly slowing the rate of conversion. Neither the filing of master deeds nor the sale of individual units has slowed significantly since the ban was adopted, as can be seen from data in Chapter 4. Presumably, as long as developers have a good prospect of selling all or most of their units without evictions, the eviction ban will not seriously deter them from converting. Analysis of our telephone sample suggests some reasons why this prospect is still good.

On average, 23 percent of the tenants in our sample (mostly longer-erm residents) purchased units in their buildings. The average rental building experiences a 40–50 percent turnover every two years—that is, particularly in the higher rent buildings that are more attractive for conversion, half or more of the tenants may move of their own accord during any two-year period. Since there is relatively little overlap between these two groups, it would appear that developers of attractive buildings could count on either selling or getting access to about 70 percent of the units during a two-year period. Given the distress that the work associated with rehabilitating a building causes tenants, an additional number of tenants might move simply to escape this unpleasantness.

It also seems likely that developers will legitimately be able to raise rents after the conversion process is well along. After conversion, the town will assess the building as a condominium once 50 percent of the units are sold. The result, as noted above, is higher taxes, the cost of which can currently be passed along in higher rents to remaining tenants. Additionally, the developer or the new unit owner may try to increase rents to recover improvement or ownership costs. Thus higher rents may serve as additional pressure for tenants to move. If all of these factors are still insufficient to make units vacant, some developers, as noted in Chapter 5, use various threatening tactics to force tenants to leave.

In the last analysis, if a few tenants in a building want to stay in it even with higher rents, the developer may be content to go along with their desires. The prospect of being able to sell the units at some future time at a significantly higher price than the original offering price (given the current market) and of having tenants paying higher rents in the interim, is acceptable to some developers. A number of converted buildings in Brookline have kept a few rental units for several years after conversion.

The May 1979 eviction ban was not aimed directly at regulating the rate of conversion; thus it is not surprising that controlling that rate is not one of its consequences. There are, however, alternative measures that could more directly affect the rate of conversions in Brookline. Some communities have banned all conversions when the vacancy rate for all apartments in the community fell below a certain level, an approach also based on the housing emergency concept that lay behind Brookline's original rent control statute. Another approach, tried in New York, is to require a high percentage of tenants in a building— say 65 percent—to agree to conversion before the owner is allowed to file a master deed.

It is not the function of this study to catalog and analyze the merits of various approaches to controlling the rate of condominium conversion.[1] The examples mentioned above are presented simply to suggest that if Brookline wished to control the rate of conversion more effectively, the means to do so are available. Given this fact, it is evident that the manner in which condominiums are regulated in Brookline can have a very significant impact on the rate at which buildings are converted. Put another way, any projection of future rates of conversion implicitly includes some assumption about how Brookline will regulate conversions.

Models of Future Tax Impacts

To estimate the future impacts of conversions on Brookline's property tax base, some assumptions about the future rate of conversions are required. As noted, there are numerous factors affecting this rate, most of which are unquantifiable. But while the future cannot be predicted with any assurance, it can be illuminated by considering the consequences of some plausible assumptions about what future rates of conversions may be like. In this section we propose two such hypothetical models.

Hypothetical Rates of Conversion

The appropriate starting point for making estimates concerning future conversion rates is the recent rate of condominium unit sales and building conversions. These data are summarized in Chapter 4. The monthly rate of both building conversions and unit sales increased sharply after activity resumed in the condominium market in 1977. Due to the effects of the 1974–1975 recession on the real estate market, there was virtually no activity in the condominium market during

---

[1] See U.S. Department of Housing and Urban Development, Division of Policy Studies, *The Conversion of Rental Housing to Condominiums and Cooperatives: A National Study of Scope, Causes and Impacts* (Washington, D.C., 1980), Chapters XI and XII, for a detailed examination of current regulatory approaches.

1974 and 1975. Subsequently, activity in Brookline began slowly, starting in May 1977 and rapidly increasing thereafter. Over the ensuing 25-month period (May 1977–July 1979), 1306 units were converted. The average monthly rate of conversion over this period (the rate at which master deeds for buildings were filed) thus was 52 units. During the same period, approximately 1435 units were sold. The average monthly selling rate of converted units was, therefore, 57 units. The difference between the rate of conversion and the rate of sales is presumably due largely to resales and perhaps to some backlog of unsold units dating from before May 1977.

Starting from this historical data, hypotheses about future rates of conversion can be established. *Hypothesis 1* will assume a monthly conversion/selling rate (net of resales) of 55, or 660 units per year. This model is also based on the following assumptions:

- Over the most typical historical 12-month period, July 1978–June 1979, the monthly selling rate was 61. If 10 percent of these sales were resales, the net selling rate was 55 units per month.
- Even though the net selling rate in the July–September 1979 period was significantly higher than 55, this higher rate should be considered a short-term anticipation of expected credit restrictions and of further regulatory restrictions on conversion.
- While future credit restrictions may temporarily retard condominium sales, an unsatisfied demand for condominiums will build up and will result in proportionately higher sales once credit eases. In other words, 55 units per month will be assumed to be the average sustainable long-term selling rate.
- The supply of buildings and units attractive for conversion remaining in Brookline will be sufficient to satisfy the demand for condominiums over the next five years.
- Any new regulations relating to conversion will not significantly discourage the conversion or sale of condominiums.

Hypothesis 2 is based on a declining monthly selling rate over the next five years. This model assumes that the monthly selling rate will decline from the current level to virtually no activity at the end of five years, as shown in Table 7.2. This model is also based on the following assumptions:

- Despite tight credit during 1980, enough money will be available to satisfy the recent average level of demand for condominiums.
- The supply of buildings appropriate for conversion will decrease

Table 7.2   Monthly Unit Selling Rate Under Hypothesis 2, 1980–1984

	January Rate	December Rate	Average Monthly Rate
1980	60	40	50
1981	30	16	23
1982	14	10	12
1983	10	6	8
1984	6	2	4

markedly, and this supply shortage will increasingly restrict sales.

- If new conversion regulations are adopted, they will gradually restrict but not prohibit conversion.
- A selling rate of about 25 units per year will be the minimum sustainable level in light of the assumed availability of buildings and the effects of new regulations.

Under Hypothesis 1, 3300 units would be sold between January 1, 1980, and December 31, 1984; under Hypothesis 2, 1164 units would be sold in the same period. As of July 1979, 1739 rent controlled units had been converted. Assume that by December 31, 1979, this number had risen to 2000. Thus under Hypothesis 1, of the approximately 11,000–12,000 units that were under rent control in 1971 (including about 9,000 still under rent control in 1979 and the 2,000 that will have been converted by 1985 under Hypothesis 1) about 46 percent will have been converted by 1985; under Hypothesis 2, about 27 percent will have been converted.

Tax Implications Conversion Models

In order to translate this hypothetical number of conversions into property tax yields, some additional assumptions about the pre-conversion rental ranges and the price distribution of converted units are necessary. These assumptions are explained in the notes to Table 7.3, and the results of the calculations are shown in the table itself.

The gross tax impacts of continued conversion under the assumptions used here are noteworthy, although they are not large in their total effect. The gross tax impact of Hypothesis 1 is about $1.4 million, or about $14.4 million in added valuations. Since under this model the total effect of revaluation would not be felt until 1984, the impact on the tax rate cannot accurately be gauged in relation to the 1979 tax. For sake of illustration, however, an increase in valuations of $14.4

Table 7.3 Property Tax Impacts of Hypothetical Conversion Rates, 1980–1984 (all data in 1979 dollars)

HYPOTHESIS 1

Price Range	Number of Units	Number of Buildings[3]	Pre-Conversion Taxes[6]	Post-Conversion Taxes[5]	Increased Taxes
High[2]					
Average Rent = $371[4]	1485	41	$2,082,946	$2,791,147	$ 708,201
Medium[2]					
Average Rent = $319[4]	1155	67	$1,381,169	$1,850,767	$ 469,598
Low[2]					
Average Rent = $281[4]	660	57	$ 688,268	$ 922,280	$ 234,012
TOTAL	3300[1]	165	$4,152,383	$5,564,194	$1,411,811

HYPOTHESIS 2

Price Range	Number of Units	Number of Buildings[3]	Pre-Conversion Taxes[6]	Post-Conversion Taxes[5]	Increased Taxes
High[2]					
Average Rent = $371[4]	524	14	$ 735,132	$ 985,077	$ 249,945
Medium[2]					
Average Rent = $319[4]	407	24	$ 486,581	$ 652,019	$ 165,438
Low[2]					
Average Rent = $281[4]	233	20	$ 243,016	$ 325,642	$ 82,626
TOTAL	1164[1]	58	$1,464,729	$1,962,738	$ 498,009

[1] Total number of units converted under Hypotheses 1 and 2, as explained in text.
[2] Distribution of high-, medium-, and low-priced units is derived from our sample of 21 buildings, as noted in Chapter 3, and also from an examination of Rent Control Board records (see Appendix C). Of the total number of units, 45% are assumed to be high-priced, 35% medium-priced, and 20% low-priced.
[3] Total number of buildings converted is derived from the total number of units converted based on average number of units per building in each price range. Average for all conversions in Brookline is 20.
[4] Average rent for each price range is derived from the sample of 21 converted buildings.
[5] Post-conversion valuations and taxes are calculated in relation to average rents in each price class using an empirical formula described in Appendix D.
[6] Pre-conversion valuations are estimated at 34% less than post-conversion valuations. Taxes are calculated at $98 per $1,000 of assessed valuation, the 1979 tax rate.

million in relation to the 1980 real estate valuation of $433 million would have reduced the 1980 tax rate by about $3.15. Similarly, Hypothesis 2 would produce about $498,000 in new taxes, increased valuations of about $5.2 million, and a resulting reduction in the 1980 tax rate of about $1.16.

In making calculations of this sort, it is always necessary to note that the estimated effects are based on the assumption that other factors will remain constant. Some of the things assumed to remain constant in estimating tax impacts are the following: (1) The relative proportion of high-, medium-, and low-priced units among all units sold will not change in the future. This assumption would be most likely to hold if the type or price range of units previously converted primarily had been a function of market demand and if the mix and financial resources of people seeking to buy condominiums did not change significantly in the future. (2) The general price level of available units will not change. The average price of units sold, as noted in Chapter 2, has not significantly changed since 1977. But a tightening of credit, causing a softening of demand, or an increase in relative demand caused by a diminished supply could affect recent price levels. (3) There will be no large increase in tax defaults or tax abatements for condominiums which will reduce actual tax yields. (4) Current tax valuation and assessment procedures will not change.

The foregoing calculation does not take into account likely increases in tax yields from rent controlled buildings which would result from general or special rent increases the Rent Control Board might allow over the next five years. The net increase in actual tax yields resulting from conversion should be adjusted to take account of likely increases in tax yields that would have taken place even if the buildings had not been converted.

One of the important factors held constant in the foregoing calculation is the present system of tax valuation and assessment. It would be useful to know how the 100 percent valuation and property classification system recently enacted in Massachusetts is likely to affect the magnitude of tax increases projected to arise from conversion. A number of factors, however, make such an estimate infeasible at this time. The primary source of uncertainty in making such estimates is the uncertain effects of new laws relating to property taxation. Recent legislation (passed in mid-1980) made major changes in the existing 100 percent valuation/property classification system. The new system is complex, and its effects cannot be estimated for only a few buildings or for only one type of property without having information about new valuations for all real property in the town.

Even under state's previous 100 percent system, which was never put into effect, it is difficult to specify the likely tax impacts of revaluation without better information than is available. The essence of the previous property valuation system was the establishment of the fair market value of all real property. Because condominium sales prices bear a determinable relationship to pre-conversion rents, it is possible to estimate the future fair market value of currently unconverted buildings (as has been done in Table 7.2) as long as it is assumed that fair market value and selling price are generally equivalent. No similar relationship between current rents of apartment buildings and their fair market value is derivable, however. Selling prices of apartment buildings could provide such an indication, but most apartment buildings in Brookline have been sold for conversion and there is evidence that many of the recorded sales prices are not truly arms-length transactions. Thus, these prices are not reliable guides to estimating the fair market value of rental property.

Because the effects of the previous 100 percent valuation can be at least roughly estimated, however, it may be useful by way of illustration to calculate the likely effects of conversion under this system. A broad analysis of this system suggests that it would have had only a minor impact on the tax benefits resulting from conversion. On the one hand, the $5,000 abatement per residence the law provided would probably have applied to every unit in a converted building rather than applying just once to the building as a whole, thus reducing the total valuation of condominiums. On the other hand, because this system based residential taxes on 40 percent of market value, apartments in Brookline would have decreased in valuation relative to condominiums. This is because apartments were valued on average at 60 percent of fair market value, based on the Town Assessor's estimate. In contrast, condominiums were assessed at 43 percent, based on the sales prices of our sample of converted buildings.

In sum, because the mechanics of the new tax valuation system are still uncertain, the actual tax consequences of conversion cannot be reliably estimated. Under the most recently used valuation procedures, however, the gross impact on the tax rate of continued conversion is 1–3 percent, depending on the assumed rate of conversion.

Budgetary Implications of Continued Conversion

While Hypotheses 1 and 2 provide some basis for considering the tax revenue impacts of continued conversion, other budgetary impacts of conversion must be considered as well. As described in Chapter 6, the characteristics of condominium households differ from those of renter households. The differences in household size, composition, age, and economic characteristics of the population resulting from continued conversion would result in some changes in demand for municipal services.

Effects on School Costs

The most significant and most obvious change in municipal services demand produced by conversion would be caused by the increase in the proportion of pre-school and school-age children per household. In our sample of renters there was an average of 0.19 pre-school and school age children per household, whereas among condominium owners the average was 0.33. In other words, for every 100 households of condominium owners who replaced 100 households of renters, there would be 14 additional school age children ($33 - 19 = 14$), an increase of 74 percent.

These ratios can be projected onto our two hypotheses, with the following results. Under Hypothesis 1, 3300 renter households would be replaced by an equal number of condominium owners over five years. Based on our sample (see Table 6.17), the renters would have a total of 706 school age children and the condominium owners (see Table 6.2) 1142, an increase of 436. Under Hypothesis 2, the comparable numbers are 249 for renters and 403 for owners, resulting in an increase of 154. These figures represent cumulative increases over a five-year period.

The total number of additional "pupil years" under Hypothesis 1 would be 1308 (one fifth of the total the first year, two fifths the second year, and so on, all cumulated). Under Hypothesis 2 the comparable pupil years would be 632.[2] Satisfactory data for estimating the cost of these additional students are not available for Brookline. Among the

---

[2] 51.6 percent the first year, 23.79 percent the second, 12.4 percent the third, 8.2 percent the fourth, and 4.1 percent the fifth. (A pupil year represents a year of school for one child. Thus a student in school from grade 1 through grade 12 represents 12 pupil years.)

data that are available are those for per-pupil expenditures—that is, the average cost of each pupil arrived at by dividing total school costs by the number of pupils. Per-pupil costs include capital expenditures, such as the debt on school buildings, as well as overhead costs such as the costs of heating schools, costs that generally do not increase when students are added. In other words, as students are added to a school system, they add only incremental or marginal costs, not average costs. The marginal costs of additional students vary depending on the number of students added. If one student is added to a class, for instance, the marginal cost is basically that of the books and the supplies (such as assignment sheets) consumed by the student. But if 30 students are added to one elementary school, an additional teacher may have to be hired. Thus, average costs greatly overstate the costs of adding students.

Marginal cost data, however, are not readily available for the types of calculations required here. For illustrative purposes only, therefore, the following calculations are presented, based on average costs. Using the 1979 per pupil expenditure of the Brookline schools, $2472, the estimated increases in students would in 1984 result in increased expenditures of $1,077,792 under Hypothesis 1 and $380,688 under Hypothesis 2. Over the five-year period, the increased number of pupil years would cost (based on the 1979 average) $3.2 million under Hypothesis 1 and $1.6 million under Hypothesis 2.

For comparison, if the 1979 school appropriation of $17.2 million were repeated for five years, the cost of the additional pupil years would be about $85.9 million. Since school costs generally are not thought of in terms of five-year units, the average annual expenditure over the five years was also calculated. Under the above assumptions this figure would be $647,664 for 262 students under Hypothesis 1 and $311,472 for 126 students under Hypothesis 2.

Discussions with the Brookline Planning Department suggest that an increasing proportion of households moving into Brookline for the first time—though not necessarily moving into condominiums—may be households with children. Since our data represented only one point in time, we have no basis for testing this impression. If this impression is correct, however, the net effect of replacing condominium households with renter households would be even smaller in terms of adding children than we have estimated.

Given these considerations, it is difficult to estimate with much precision what the net budgetary impact—considering both increased tax yields and increased school costs—of either hypothetical rate of conversion would be. It is quite certain, however, that the average net tax benefit to the town would be substantially larger than the $764,147 that is the result of subtracting the average annual increased school cost based on per-pupil expenditures ($647,664) from the average annual increased tax yield under Hypothesis 1 ($1,411,811) or the net figure of $186,627 arrived at under Hypothesis 2.

Other Effects on Municipal Service Demand

In terms of Brookline's annual budget, increased school costs would be by far the most significant effect of the difference in household characteristics between renters and condominium owners. One other measurable cost impact, however, could result from the decreased household size of condominium owners as compared to renters. The average household size for renters in our sample was 2.05 whereas the comparable figure for condominium owners was 1.95, a decrease in household size of 4.9 percent. Thus, based on our sample, the 3300 condominium households in Hypothesis 1 would contain a total of 6,435 people. These people would replace 6,765 people if the units had been rented and had contained the average sample size of renter households—a decrease of 330 people. The comparable figures for Hypothesis 2 are 2,270 in condominium households and 2,386 in rental households, a decrease of 116.

There is no reliable way to estimate the decrease in municipal costs attributable to these decreases in population. Average per capita costs for all town services are even less meaningful than average per pupil costs for school services. An idea of the relative impact of these small numbers on town services can be seen by noting that 330 people represent 0.6 percent of the 1978 Brookline population of 57,016, whereas 116 people represent 0.2 percent. A decrease this small is not likely to cause a noticeable impact on most town services. Water consumption, sewer usage, and trash collection would probably decrease by small, if measurable, amounts. The magnitude of these decreases, however, would be considerably less in absolute terms than the offsetting increases in school costs.

Finally, it may be asked whether other characteristics that distinguish condominium households from rental households would cause any noticeable impact on the demand for town services. As described in Chapter 6, condominium households tend to have larger incomes, are more likely to be married, and are on average somewhat older than renter households. It is not apparent that any of these characteristics is significantly correlated with either a more or less intense use of municipal services. More detailed household surveys or future experience may reveal that condominium households use public library facilities less or more, call for police assistance less or more, or differ in other ways from renters in their use of municipal services. No evidence is presently available, however.

Our overall conclusion—that the largest impact on town services of a change in household characteristics is on the school system—is in general in agreement with the conclusions of Brookline's 1976 "Report of the Housing Study Committee." The housing study committee inquired into the impacts on town services of subsidized housing and into the different types of households that live in different kinds of such housing. Aside from a minor increase in demand for services for the elderly (a factor not applicable in our study), the committee also concluded that school costs were the only town expenses significantly affected by changes in household characteristics.

Questions about the impact of condominiums upon their neighborhoods have also been raised. The issue may be addressed in two ways: Do people who live in condominiums have an adverse or a positive influence in their immediate neighborhoods? Or, is building maintenance positively or adversely influenced by its status as a condominium?

The differences in personal or household characteristics (such as age, income, occupation, marital status, and number of children) between renter and condominium households have been analyzed earlier. There is no objective standard by which these changes can be judged desirable or undesirable. Nor is there any evidence that the types of households attracted by condominiums in Brookline are more prone to conduct that is generally deemed anti-social, such as committing crimes, engaging in loud and disturbing behavior, or the like, than are the renter households they replace.

A concentration of condominiums in a neighborhood is likely to have an impact on the types of people living in that neighborhood because of the changes in household characteristics described in Chapter 6. Figure 4.1, a map showing the location of condominiums in Brookline, reveals a number of such clusters. Whether the changes resulting from such concentrations are desirable is, again, a subject to which no objective standards can be applied.

Because the household income of condominium owners is higher than that of renters, owners have additional disposable income, some of which is likely to be spent in Brookline. In a neighborhood in which condominiums are concentrated, this additional disposable income may have an impact on stores located in the neighborhood; more generally, it may result in higher sales in all Brookline stores. Since our interviewees were asked no questions about spending or buying patterns, however, we have no basis on which to estimate the magnitude of the additional spending stream or the types of goods, services, or stores that may be affected.

Solid evidence with regard to the upkeep of buildings by condominium owners is not yet in. Generally, a developer will make at least minor improvements to a building's appearance at the time of conversion—for instance, painting or adding landscaping—if such improvements are needed. The more important question, however, is whether the new owners will properly maintain the building's appearance and condition. We have heard no complaints about buildings converted before 1975, which have been maintained by condominium associations for several years. The condominium market changed drastically in 1977, however, and we have looked for concrete evidence of the more recent owners' attitudes.

The most tangible evidence on maintenance available is the amount of money the new owners assess themselves for building maintenance as compared to what the previous landlord spent. We collected data from 10 buildings that had detailed audited operating costs on record with the Rent Control Board (the costs were on record because the buildings' owners had at some time requested special rent increases). For these buildings we obtained the condominium operating budgets from their current trustees. A comparison of these data was then attempted.

The overall impression we gained from comparing the data was that no dramatic changes, either up or down, had been made in the amounts spent on building maintenance. This conclusion is tentative, though, because in many ways we were comparing unlike quantities. In a condominium, unit owners maintain the interiors of their units— supplying paint, fixtures, appliances, plumbing, repairs, and so on. When the condominiums were apartment buildings, these costs were the landlords' responsibility. Many condominiums do not have full-time janitorial service but must make arrangements to secure these services previously provided and paid for by landlords. Then too, the operating data for the buildings as apartment buildings predate the condominium data by three to eight years (in our sample), and the precise effects of inflation on these earlier reported costs are hard to measure accurately. When all of these factors are taken into account and noncomparable costs such as apartment house mortgage payments are filtered out, it does not appear that the pre- and post-conversion maintenance expenditures show any consistent pattern of much higher or much lower spending.

Drastic changes in building maintenance either up or down following the conversion of a building might have some impact on town services, such as increased rubbish removal needs or decreased likelihood of fire. Our data, however, provide no support for a finding one way or the other. In sum, therefore, there is little documentable evidence concerning the character of impacts that conversions have on a neighborhood.

Chapter 8

RESOLVING PUBLIC POLICY ISSUES RAISED BY CONVERSION

This study originated in Brookline's concern about the effects large-scale conversion might have on the town. The issues raised by conversion are real and complex; they pose difficult social, economic, and political choices about where the public interest lies. To sort out these choices and to formulate an appropriate local policy toward conversion requires an understanding of what groups are involved in conversion, what their interests are, and what the consequences of their actions are likely to be.

The major issues surrounding large-scale conversion at the local level arise from three types of conflicts:

- The conflict between would-be purchasers of condominiums and renters who are displaced involuntarily.
- The conflict between developers who want to convert and tenants who want to continue to rent.
- The conflict between the lure of increased property tax revenues and the disruption of the status quo large-scale conversion can bring.

In deciding how to address the condominium issue, a community must decide, implicitly or explicitly, how to balance these conflicting interests. What information does a community need to enable it to resolve these conflicts?

Would-Be Condominium Purchasers vs. Tenants

To deal with the conflict between would-be purchasers and potential displaced tenants, it is essential to understand the types of households involved and their housing needs and wants. It is generally true, in Brookline and elsewhere, that condominium owners tend to be somewhat better off economically than the renters they replace. But in terms of public policy, it is critical to know how wide this economic gap is and what the income level of the renters being displaced is. If the buildings being converted contain high rent luxury units, the renters who choose not to buy probably have a good chance of finding acceptable housing elsewhere at a price they can afford. While the tenants may well be unhappy about being forced to make such a move-or-buy decision, in most instances they will probably have the economic resources to cope with the vagaries of the housing market without special assistance from local government.

When pre-conversion rents and tenants are in the low-to-moderate price/income range, however, the situation is quite different. Unless there is a good supply of subsidized housing available, lower income renters may well have a difficult time finding affordable comparable housing without moving a considerable distance. This observation follows from the finding that conversion is most likely to take place in strong housing markets in which demand is at least equal to if not greater than supply. It would be unlikely in such circumstances to find a good supply of lower-priced rental units.

Income, of course, is not the only important consideration in analyzing the relationship between buyers and renters. Relocation for the elderly, many of whom in Brookline have spend many years in the same building or neighborhood, is particularly traumatic. In addition, the persons comprising many older households in Brookline are the parents of other town residents. Thus the prospect of confronting these people with an unwanted move had a negative effect on residents and their extended families and considerably heightened the emotional content of the conversion issue. Understanding that such a situation exists is important for any community, but creating more housing for the elderly is probably the only way to alleviate it if the conversion process is allowed to run its course.

While the difficulties experienced by low income or elderly households that are forced to relocate are very real, it is important to determine the magnitude of this problem in establishing local policies. The normal turnover of rental apartments will substantially diminish the number of households that face difficult move-or-buy decisions. Medium- and high-priced rental buildings—those most likely to be converted—experience on average a 20–25 percent or more turnover each year. Although such turnover will not diminish the trauma of conversion for long-term tenants, it will substantially reduce the number of renters directly affected.

While it is perhaps natural to focus on how current renters are threatened by conversion, the interests of would-be purchasers are also a significant consideration. More than half of all condominium purchasers, both in Brookline and in similar communities nationwide, are residents of the community, either as renters in units they subsequently purchased or as residents elsewhere in town. These buyers are most frequently younger households for whom condominium purchase is the only realistic way into the homeowning market. The rapid escalation of housing prices, particularly in the very communities where large-scale conversion reflects a strong housing market, has in effect forced these households to remain renters and forego the psychological and economic benefits of home ownership. Tenant groups, which often represent lower income households, may take the view that the economic status of these households is not such as to merit any special consideration from their communities. The opposing view might argue, on the other hand, that any intervention in the housing market to protect low income, elderly, or other economically vulnerable groups from the conversion process is nevertheless an action against other community residents for whom condominiums are the only available route to home ownership.

The remedies available to a community facing large-scale conversion range from controlling the rate of conversion, to increasing the amount of low-income or elderly housing, to subsidizing the purchase of condominiums by low-income tenants. Our purpose here is not to weigh the appropriateness of varying remedies but simply to underline how important it is to have good information about the types and numbers of renters moving out as a result of conversion and about the types, numbers, and locations of households seeking to buy condominiums. The types of detailed survey data collected for this study is critical to making informed social policies in this difficult area.

A useful adjunct to this type of data is the housing cost/income analysis carried out in Chapter 6. The effects of inflation, both on current income and on the future value of current housing investments, have invalidated many of the old rules of thumb about what type of housing is affordable at different income levels. The model presented in Chapter 6 presents a way of translating current rents paid into the net costs of owning the same unit as a condominium. In place of requiring local officials to make value judgments about what is an appropriate portion of income to spend on housing, this approach simply relates current rents to the price range of currently available condominiums. Having this knowledge, a community is better equipped to judge how difficult the economic choice of buying rather than renting is. Tax advantages notwithstanding, the conversion of a rental unit to a condominium will inevitably raise the occupant's monthly housing cost. By translating current rentals into expected condominium carrying costs (based on current market data), a community can determine at what rent level condominium ownership is likely to become too great a cost to bear. Correlating these data with knowledge of the income structure of current renter households will reveal the proportion of tenants for whom the move-or-buy choice is economically unfeasible and therefore will also reveal what groups should properly be the focus of public policy.

Building Owners vs. Tenants

A second type of conflict a community facing a wave of conversions must confront is the struggle between tenants and building owners. Whereas the conflict between renters and would-be purchasers is a sort of guerrilla warfare carried on in individual hand-to-hand encounters, the struggle between renters and building owners is more often a pitched battle fought in a deafening rhetorical uproar. Building owners are an identifiable group, often with professional associations to back them up. Tenants often respond in kind by creating their own interest groups. The rhetoric is familiar and usually bombastic. Owners portray the right to a fair profit on investment and to dispose of assets as they wish, within the law, as the essence of free enterprise and the basis of the nation's economic strength; juxtaposed to these claims are the tenants' assertions of their rights to security in their homes at reasonable rents.

The claims of both owners and tenants need to be examined. Regarding the tenant's view, it is important to understand how conversion is taking place: the type of building being converted, the kinds of tenants who choose to buy and the kinds who leave, how much notice the owner provides, whether the owner offers any assistance in finding a new apartment, and whether the owner deals fairly with tenants during the conversion process.

Regarding the owner's view, it is important to understand the financial structure of building conversion. A model for analyzing the relationship among the developer's investment, risk, and expected profit is presented in Chapter 3. When a developer's risk is high—for instance, because of large rehabilitation costs or a slow rate of unit sales—it can be expected that tenants will be subjected to increasing pressure to move out if they choose not to buy. Typically, it is this sort of situation that will force some tenants to move out under circumstances likely to attract media coverage and inflame tenant-owner relations. In low-risk situations, it is usually to the developer's advantage to keep a lower profile, perhaps thereby extending the conversion process but also avoiding unwanted publicity.

Since condominium conversion is, from a developer's viewpoint, simply another form of real estate investment, the reasonableness of a developer's profit can be appropriately judged in relation to investment yields elsewhere in the real estate market. In Brookline, the average profit margin—the return on the total investment made in the conversion—appeared to be about 20 percent, and the return on the developer's own investment (equity) appeared to range between 20 and 30 percent, when figured over a two- to three-year period (see Chapter 3). In relation to other opportunities for real estate investment in the Boston area, these figures appeared to be reasonable. These figures, however, will vary in different markets, and communities should make their own analyses to determine whether developers are making returns on conversions that are in line with their risks and with expectations in local real estate markets.

Increased Property Tax Revenues vs. Disruption of the Status Quo

Finally, a community must consider the potential conflict between anticipated property tax revenue increases resulting from conversion and other effects of large-scale conversion on the community's well-being. The property tax effects of conversion, both in Brookline and nationwide, are significant enough to be measurable but have not yet had a major effect on local tax rates. How much a building's assessment will increase after conversion depends heavily on local assessing practices. In Brookline, for instance, the tax assessor has in the past implicitly distinguished between income properties, including apartment rentals, and single family owner-occupied residences. Recent property tax reform legislation in Massachusetts may require, however, that all residential property be taxed on the same basis. In the past, Brookline's practices produced an increase of about one third in post-conversion valuations, but this may now change.

Aside from the change in the form of residential ownership, most conversions also involve some added investment in the property in question, often extending beyond basic maintenance to significant improvements in units or common areas. The investment represented by adding a swimming pool or remodeling all of a building's kitchens and bathrooms should be reflected in higher unit market values and higher assessments and thus in increased tax revenues.

Tax increases resulting from conversion, in Brookline or elsewhere, have not generally been large enough to have had a major effect on property tax rates. Even in Brookline, which has had a very high rate of conversions, the roughly 2,000 units converted (which represented 15–16 percent of the 1971 rent controlled apartments) represent only 7–8 percent of all housing units and represent a much smaller percentage of the total current assessed value of residential property. Thus, even the effects of large-scale conversion and fairly substantial post-conversion assessment increases were heavily diluted by the larger proportion of other residential assessments. The net property tax increase in Brookline directly traceable to conversion has probably been 1–3 percent, a figure within the range identified nationwide by the recent Department of Housing and Urban Development study.[1]

Offsetting increases in the demand for municipal services resulting from conversion are not generally evident. Communities should probably focus most on changes in the numbers of school age children associated with conversion. Conversion has not markedly changed the socioeconomic character of most (though not all) neighborhoods; thus,

---

[1] U.S. Department of Housing and Urban Development, Division of Policy Studies, *The Conversion of Rental Housing to Condominiums and Cooperatives: A National Study of Scope, Causes and Impacts* (Washington, D.C., 1980), pp. VIII-2–VIII-11.

aside from changes in the demand for public school spaces, a community is not likely to have to respond in any major way to conversion in terms of the services it provides.

What does seem fairly clear on the record of the last few years, however, is that the conversion of a substantial number of apartment buildings to condominiums will stir up a community, change the status quo in terms of who lives in the community, affect the balance between property owners and renters, and in consequence raise a broad range of difficult issues for the community to confront and a series of conflicts for it to resolve. Understanding the character of these changes and knowing how to get at the facts behind the conflicts will better equip a community to develop policies appropriate to the issues large-scale conversion creates.

Appendix A

STUDY QUESTIONNAIRES

Project #4361

Interviewing begins: 8/29/79

RENT CONTROL TENANTS

Hello, I'm calling from Becker
Research Corporation of Boston.
We're doing a survey for the
town selectmen in Brookline
in order to get people's reactions and concerns about
the conversion of apartments
to condominiums, and I'd like
to speak to the head of the
household.

INTERVIEWER: DO NOT COMPLETE

I.D.#

```
__COL. 1  1 2 3 4 5 6 7 8 9 0
__COL. 2  1 2 3 4 5 6 7 8 9 0
__COL. 3  1 2 3 4 5 6 7 8 9 0
__COL. 4  1 2 3 4 5 6 7 8 9 0
__COL. 5  1 2 3 4 5 6 7 8 9 0
```

INTERVIEWER: COMPLETE

COL. 8   1 MALE   2 FEMALE

---

1 To begin with, about how
   long have you lived in
   Brookline?

COL. 9

1 0-5 MONTHS
2 6-11 MONTHS
3 1 YEAR UP TO 2 YEARS
4 2 YEARS UP TO 5 YEARS
5 5 YEARS UP TO 10 YEARS
6 10 YEARS OR MORE
7 DON'T KNOW

---

2 How long have you lived
   in this apartment?

COL. 10

1 LESS THAN 1 MONTH
2 1-3 MONTHS
3 4-6 MONTHS
4 7-12 MONTHS
5 13-18 MONTHS
6 19-24 MONTHS
7 25-36 MONTHS
8 3-5 YEARS
9 MORE THAN 5 YEARS
0 DON'T KNOW/REFUSED

---

3 Have you previously owned
   a house?

COL. 11

1 YES
2 NO
3 DON'T KNOW

---

4 Do you plan to move in the
   near future? (within the
   next year)?

COL. 12

1 YES
2 NO
3 DON'T KNOW

		COL. 13	COL. 14
5	What are the three things you like most about your present apartment?		

COL. 13

1 I HAVE FRIENDS
   IN THE BUILDING
2 I LIKE THE NEIGH-
   BORHOOD
3 I'M CLOSE TO
   WHERE I WORK
4 THE BUILDING
   HAS A LOT OF
   AMENITIES
5 I CAN AFFORD THE
   RENTAL COST
6 I'M CLOSE TO PUB-
   LIC TRANSPORTA-
   TION
7 I LIKE THE WAY
   THE BUILDING IS
   MANAGED
8 GOOD SCHOOLS
9 GOOD SERVICES IN
   TOWN (FIRE,
   POLICE, ETC.)
0 OTHER_____
   (SPECIFY)
X DON'T KNOW

COL. 14

1
2
3
4
5
6
7
8
9
0
X
Y

---

6 As you may know, several apartment buildings in Brookline have been converted to condominiums. Have you heard anything about possible plans to convert your building from rental units to condominiums?

COL. 15   SKIP TO

1 YES   7
2 NO   9
3 DON'T KNOW   9

---

7 Has your building been converted?

COL. 16

1 YES
2 NO
3 DON'T KNOW

---

8 What are your reactions to what you have heard?

COL. 17	COL. 18
1	1
2	2
3	3
4	4
5	5
6	6
7	7
8	8
9	9
0	0
X	X
Y	Y

9	If your building were con- verted to condominium units, would you consider purchasing the unit or would you prefer to stay as a tenant under the protection of the current eviction ban or would you move out?	COL. 19		SKIP TO
		1	CONSIDER PUR- CHASING	11
		2	PREFER TO STAY AS TENANT UNDER PROTECTION	11
		3	WOULD MOVE OUT	10
		4	DON'T KNOW	11

10	Why would you move out?	COL. 20		COL. 21
		1	I AM TOO OLD TO BUY A CONDO- MINIUM	1 2 3
		2	A CONDOMINIUM WOULD BE TOO EXPENSIVE FOR ME	4 5 6 7
		3	I DON'T WANT TO OWN A CONDO- MINIUM	8 9 0
		4	THIS BUILDING HAS PROBLEMS	X Y
		5	I DON'T WANT TO LIVE IN THIS NEIGHBORHOOD	
		6	A CONDOMINIUM IS A BAD INVEST- MENT	
		7	OTHER_____ (SPECIFY)	
		8	DON'T KNOW	

11	If your apartment were to be converted to a condo- minium unit, under what conditions, if any, would you consider buying it?	COL. 22	COL. 23
		1	1
		2	2
		3	3
		4	4
		5	5
		6	6
		7	7
		8	8
		9	9
		0	0
		X	X
		Y	Y

12	Has the owner of your build- ing ever tried to evict you from your unit so that it could be converted to a condominium?	COL. 24		SKIP TO
		1	YES	14
		2	NO	13
		3	DON'T KNOW	13

13	Has your landlord ever tried to harass you because he/she wanted to convert your unit to a condominium?	COL. 25		SKIP TO
		1	YES	20
		2	NO	21
		3	DON'T KNOW	21

14	How much time were you given to vacate the unit?	COL. 26	
		1	LESS THAN 1 WEEK
		2	1 WEEK-1 MONTH
		3	MORE THAN 1 MONTH-3 MONTHS
		4	MORE THAN 3 MONTHS-6 MONTHS
		5	MORE THAN 6 MONTHS
		6	DON'T KNOW

15	Do you feel you were given adequate advance notice, that is, enough lead time to find suitable replacement housing?	COL. 27	
		1	YES
		2	NO
		3	DON'T KNOW

16	Did your landlord offer to help you find replacement housing?	COL. 28	
		1	YES
		2	NO
		3	DON'T KNOW

17	Did he/she actually help you?	COL. 29		SKIP TO
		1	YES	18
		2	NO	19
		3	DON'T KNOW	19

18	What did he/she do to help you?	COL. 30	COL. 31
		1	1
		2	2
		3	3
		4	4
		5	5
		6	6
		7	7
		8	8
		9	9
		0	0
		X	X
		Y	Y

19	Did your landlord cause you any trouble after giving you notice to vacate?	COL. 32		SKIP TO
		1	YES	20
		2	NO	21
		3	DON'T KNOW	21

20	What did he/she do that caused you trouble?	COL. _33_	COL. _34_
		1	1
		2	2
		3	3
		4	4
		5	5
		6	6
		7	7
		8	8
		9	9
		0	0
		X	X
		Y	Y

21	Has your landlord petitioned the rent control board for an increase in the rent of your apartment during the past twelve months?	COL. _35_		SKIP TO
		1	YES	22
		2	NO	24
		3	DON'T KNOW	24

22	What was the amount of the increase he/she was asking?	COL. _36_	
		1	$10-50 PER MONTH
		2	$51-100 PER MONTH
		3	$101-150 PER MONTH
		4	MORE THAN $150 PER MONTH
		5	DON'T KNOW

23	What action did the rent control board take on your landlord's petition?	COL. _37_	
		1	NO ACTION YET
		2	RENT INCREASE DENIED
		3	RENT INCREASE GRANTED
		4	PETITION RETURNED FOR FURTHER INFORMATION
		5	BOARD REFUSED TO PROCESS PETITION
		6	OTHER_____(SPECIFY)
		7	DON'T KNOW

24	Do you have a parking space with your apartment?	COL. _38_		SKIP TO
		1	YES	25
		2	NO	27
		3	DON'T KNOW	27

25	Has your landlord attempted to take away your parking space in the last twelve months?	COL. _39_	
		1	YES
		2	NO
		3	DON'T KNOW

26	Has your landlord attempted to increase the fee you pay for your parking space in the last twelve months?	COL. _40_	
		1	YES
		2	NO
		3	DON'T KNOW

27	Has your landlord made physical improvements to your apartment during the past twelve months that you did not request?	COL. 41		SKIP TO
		1	YES	28
		2	NO	29
		3	DON'T KNOW	29

28	What kind of improvements did he/she make?	COL. 42	COL. 43
		1	1
		2	2
		3	3
		4	4
		5	5
		6	6
		7	7
		8	8
		9	9
		0	0
		X	X
		Y	Y

29	Has your landlord cut back on any services during the past twelve months?	COL. 44		SKIP TO
		1	YES	30
		2	NO	31
		3	DON'T KNOW	31

30	What services has he/she cut back on?	COL. 45	COL. 46
		1	1
		2	2
		3	3
		4	4
		5	5
		6	6
		7	7
		8	8
		9	9
		0	0
		X	X
		Y	Y

31	Has your landlord attempted to sell your apartment as a condominium during the past twelve months?	COL. 47		SKIP TO
		1	YES	32
		2	NO	35
		3	DON'T KNOW	35

32	Has he brought prospective purchasers to view your apartment in the past twelve months?	COL. 48		SKIP TO
		1	YES	33
		2	NO	35
		3	DON'T KNOW	35

33 How much advance notice has he/she usually given you before bringing prospective purchasers to see your apartment?

COL. 49

1 LESS THAN ONE DAY
2 1-2 DAYS
3 3-5 DAYS
4 6-7 DAYS
5 MORE THAN A WEEK
6 DON'T KNOW

34 How many times has he/she brought prospective purchasers to see your apartment in the past twelve months?

COL. 50

1 ONCE OR TWICE
2 3 TO 12 TIMES
3 13 TO 24 TIMES
4 MORE THAN 24 TIMES
5 DON'T KNOW

NOW I HAVE A FEW QUESTIONS FOR BACKGROUND PURPOSES ONLY.

35 How many bedrooms does your apartment ·have?

COL. 51'

1 0
2 1
3 2
4 3
5 4
6 MORE THAN 4
7 DON'T KNOW/REFUSED

36 What is your marital status? Are you:

COL. 52   INTERVIEWER: READ

1 MARRIED
2 SINGLE
3 WIDOWED
4 DIVORCED/SEPARATED
5 OTHER _____ (SPECIFY)

DO NOT READ
6 DON'T KNOW/REFUSED

37 Including yourself, how many people live in this apartment?

COL. 53

1 ONE
2 TWO
3 THREE
4 FOUR
5 FIVE OR MORE
6 DON'T KNOW/REFUSED

38 How many adults live in this apartment?

COL. 54

1 ONE
2 TWO
3 THREE
4 FOUR
5 FIVE OR MORE
6 DON'T KNOW/REFUSED

39	How many children do you have living with you?	COL. 55	SKIP TO
		0 NONE	
		1 ONE	40
		2 TWO	40
		3 THREE	40
		4 FOUR	40
		5 FIVE	40
		6 SIX	40
		7 SEVEN OR MORE	40
		8 DON'T KNOW/REFUSED	

40	How many children do you have living with you 5 years of age or under?	COL. 56
		0 NONE
		1 ONE
		2 TWO
		3 THREE
		4 FOUR
		5 FIVE
		6 SIX
		7 SEVEN OR MORE
		8 DON'T KNOW/REFUSED

41	How many children do you have living with you be-tween the ages of 6 and 19? (INCLUDES 6-YEAR-OLDS and 19-YEAR-OLDS)	COL. 57
		0 NONE
		1 ONE
		2 TWO
		3 THREE
		4 FOUR
		5 FIVE
		6 SIX
		7 SEVEN OR MORE
		8 DON'T KNOW/REFUSED

42	How many children do you have living with you 20 years of age or older?	COL. 58
		0 NONE
		1 ONE
		2 TWO
		3 THREE
		4 FOUR
		5 FIVE
		6 SIX
		7 SEVEN OR MORE
		8 DON'T KNOW/REFUSED

43	Is this a single-parent household?	COL. 59
		1 YES
		2 NO
		3 DON'T KNOW

44	Are you presently employed?	COL. 60	SKIP TO
		1 YES	45
		2 NO	46
		3 DON'T KNOW	46

45	Into which of the following job categories does your job fall?	COL. 61 INTERVIEWER: READ	SKIP TO
		1 PROFESSIONAL JOB	47
		2 TECHNICAL JOB	47
		3 MANAGERIAL JOB	47
		4 SALES JOB	47
		5 CLERICAL JOB	47
		6 OTHER _____ (SPECIFY) DO NOT READ	47
		7 DON'T KNOW/REFUSED	47

46	Are you retired?	COL. 62
		1 YES
		2 NO
		3 DON'T KNOW

47	Is your spouse (or other principal member of the household) employed?	COL. 63	SKIP TO
		1 YES	48
		2 NO	49
		3 DON'T KNOW	49

48	Into which of the following job categories does his/her job fall?	COL. 64 INTERVIEWER: READ	SKIP TO
		1 PROFESSIONAL JOB	50
		2 TECHNICAL JOB	50
		3 MANAGERIAL JOB	50
		4 SALES JOB	50
		5 CLERICAL JOB	50
		6 OTHER _____ (SPECIFY) DO NOT READ	50
		7 DON'T KNOW/REFUSED	50

49	Is he/she retired	COL. 65
		1 YES
		2 NO
		3 DON'T KNOW

50	Into which of the following categories does the total monthly rent (with utilities) for your apartment fall?	COL. 66 INTERVIEWER: READ
		1 LESS THAN $200
		2 $200-299
		3 $300-399
		4 $400-500
		5 OVER $500 DO NOT READ
		6 DON'T KNOW/REFUSED

51 Into which of the following   COL. 67   INTERVIEWER: READ
    categories does your own
    age fall?   1 UNDER 21
                                    2 21-30
                                    3 31-40
                                    4 41-50
                                    5 51-60
                                    6 61-70
                                    7 71 AND OVER
                                    DO NOT READ
                                    8 DON'T KNOW/REFUSED

52 Finally, into which of the   COL. 68   INTERVIEWER: READ
    following categories did
    your total family income   1 UNDER $10,000
    fall in 1978?   2 $10,000-19,999
                                    3 $20,000-29,999
                                    4 $30,000-39,999
                                    5 $40,000-49,999
                                    6 OVER $50,000
                                    DO NOT READ
                                    7 DON'T KNOW

53 What is the primary source   COL. 69
    of income for this house-
    hold?   1 SALARY & WAGES
                                    2 INTEREST & DIVIDENDS
                                    3 SELF-EMPLOYED
                                    4 SOCIAL SECURITY/PENSION
                                    5 PUBLIC ASSISTANCE
                                    6 TRUST FUND
                                    7 OTHER
                                    8 DON'T KNOW/REFUSED

And your address is . . .

ADDRESS_____   CITY_____ ZIP_____

TELEPHONE NUMBER_____ DATE_____

Thank respondent for his/her cooperation.

Interviewer's signature_____

DO NOT COMPLETE

          NUMBER OF UNITS IN THE BUILDING

          COL. 70   COL. 71

          1 | 7   1 | 7
          2 | 8   2 | 8
          3 | 9   3 | 9
          4 | 0   4 | 0
          5 | X   5 | X
          6 | Y   6 | Y

Project #4361   INTERVIEWER: DO <u>NOT</u> COMPLETE

Interviewing begins: I.D.#

    CONDOMINIUM OWNER

Hello, I'm calling from Becker   __COL. 1 1 2 3 4 5 6 7 8 9 0
Research Corporation of Boston.   __COL. 2 1 2 3 4 5 6 7 8 9 0
We are doing a study for the   __COL. 3 1 2 3 4 5 6 7 8 9 0
town selectmen in Brookline   __COL. 4 1 2 3 4 5 6 7 8 9 0
in order to get people's re-   __COL. 5 1 2 3 4 5 6 7 8 9 0
actions and concerns about
the conversion of apartments
to condominiums. The study is   INTERVIEWER: <u>COMPLETE</u>
among people who live in con-
verted condominiums. I would   COL._8_ 1 MALE   2 FEMALE
like to speak to the head of
the household.

1 To begin with, I would like   COL._9_
   to ask you a few questions
   about the places you lived   1 OWNED HOUSE
   before you purchased your   2 OWNED CONDOMINIUM
   condominium. Can you please   3 RENTED HOUSE
   tell me what your former   4 RENTED APARTMENT
   occupancy status was? That   5 OTHER _____ (SPECIFY)
   is, did you own your last   6 DON'T KNOW/REFUSED
   home or apartment or did
   you rent a home or apartment?

2 Where was your previous   COL._10_
   residence located?
                                      1 BROOKLINE, SAME ADDRESS
                                      2 BROOKLINE, DIFFERENT ADDRESS
                                      3 METRO BOSTON AREA BUT NOT
                                         BROOKLINE _____
                                                   (SPECIFY TOWN)
                                      4 MASSACHUSETTS BUT NOT
                                         METRO BOSTON
                                      5 OUTSIDE MASSACHUSETTS
                                      6 DON'T KNOW/REFUSED

3 Approximately how long did   COL._11_
   you live at your former
   residence before you pur-   1 UNDER 13 MONTHS
   chased your condominium?   2 13-36 MONTHS
                                      3 37 MONTHS TO 5 YEARS
                                      4 MORE THAN 5 YEARS
                                      5 DON'T KNOW/REFUSED

4	Why did you move from your previous residence to this condominium unit? PROBE (MULTIPLE RESPONSES PERMITTED)	COL. 12

1 CHANGE IN FAMILY SIZE
2 WANTED MORE ROOM
3 DISSATISFACTION WITH APART-MENT
4 DISSATISFACTION WITH BUILDING
5 DISSATISFACTION WITH LANDLORD
6 DISSATISFACTION WITH NEIGH-BORHOOD
7 DISSATISFACTION WITH OTHER TENANTS
8 RENTING BECAME TOO EXPEN-SIVE, RENT INCREASED
9 WANTED TO OWN
0 COULD AFFORD A BETTER PLACE
X LOCATION INCONVENIENT
Y CHANGED JOB

COL. 13

1 TOWN SERVICES (FIRE, POLICE)
2 BETTER SCHOOLS
3 OTHER _____(SPECIFY)
4 DON'T KNOW/REFUSED

5	What were the one or two most important factors in your decision to buy a condominium? PROBE (MULTIPLE RESPONSES PERMITTED)	COL. 14

1 GETTING A BETTER PLACE TO LIVE
2 NO   APARTMENTS OF THE RIGHT SIZE
3 NO RENTED APARTMENTS OF THE RIGHT PRICE
4 NO RENTED APARTMENTS AVAIL-ABLE IN RIGHT LOCATION
5 TAX SHELTER/SOME PROTECTION AGAINST PROPERTY TAXES
6 PREFER TO OWN (BETTER THAN RENTING)
7 WAS A GOOD INVESTMENT
8 LESS EXPENSIVE THAN RENTING (MORTGAGE PAYMENTS ARE LOWER/EQUAL TO RENT)
9 OTHER_____(SPECIFY)
0 DON'T KNOW

6	What was your primary reason for moving to your particular condominium building? (MULTIPLE RESPONSES PERMITTED)	COL. 15

1 COST OF UNIT
2 GOOD NEIGHBORHOOD
3 GOOD LOCATION FOR WORK/JOB
4 GOOD LOCATION FOR SHOPPING
5 GOOD LOCATION FOR FRIENDS
6 UNIT/BUILDING AMENITIES
7 OTHER_____(SPECIFY)
8 DON'T KNOW

7 At the time you were considering purchasing your
   current unit, were you
   also considering:

COL. 16 INTERVIEWER: READ

1 RENTING AN APARTMENT
2 RENTING A HOUSE
3 BUYING A HOUSE OR WERE YOU
4 ONLY CONSIDERING BUYING A
   CONDOMINIUM?
   DO NOT READ
5 OTHER_____ (SPECIFY)
6 DON'T KNOW

8 Approximately how long did
   you look before buying
   your condominium?

COL. 17

1 ONE MONTH OR LESS
2 MORE THAN ONE TO THREE MONTHS
3 MORE THAN THREE TO SIX MONTHS
4 MORE THAN SIX TO TWELVE MONTHS
5 MORE THAN TWELVE MONTHS
6 DON'T KNOW

9 Did you formerly rent the
   unit you currently own?

COL. 18　　　　SKIP TO

1 YES　　　　11
2 NO　　　　10
3 DON'T KNOW　10

10 Did you formerly rent another unit in the building
   in which you now live?

COL. 19　　　　SKIP TO

1 YES　　　　11
2 NO　　　　18
3 DON'T KNOW　18

11 What was your primary
   reason for purchasing
   rather than moving elsewhere?

COL. 20

1 BEST BUY/COULDN'T AFFORD
   TO MOVE
2 TOO OLD TO MOVE
3 LIKE LOCATION
4 LIKE APARTMENT
5 GOOD INVESTMENT
6 INCONVENIENCE OF MOVING
7 OTHER_____(SPECIFY)
8 DON'T KNOW

12 Did the landlord offer you
   a lower price on the unit
   than to non-tenants?

COL. 21　　　　SKIP TO

1 YES　　　　13
2 NO　　　　14
3 DON'T KNOW　14

13 How much lower?

_____
(INTERVIEWER: WRITE IN
AMOUNT)

COL. 22

1 | 7
2 | 8
3 | 9
4 | 0
5 | X
6 | Y

14	Did the landlord offer you other inducements to buy?	COL. 23	SKIP TO
		1 YES	15
		2 NO	16
		3 DON'T KNOW	16

15	What other inducements to buy did your landlord offer you?	COL. 24
		1 MORTGAGE WITH LOWER INTEREST RATES
		2 MORTGAGE WITH SMALLER DOWN PAYMENT
		3 ADDITIONAL RENOVATIONS OR IMPROVEMENTS
		4 DEFERRED DOWN PAYMENT
		5 PAYMENT OF REAL ESTATE TAXES
		6 OTHER_____(SPECIFY)
		7 DON'T KNOW

16	Did the landlord try to apply pressure to convince you to buy?	COL. 25	SKIP TO
		1 YES	17
		2 NO	18
		3 DON'T KNOW	18

17	What did he/she try to do?	COL. 26
		1 TRIED TO RAISE RENT
		2 SENT THREATENING LETTER
		3 TOOK/TRIED TO TAKE PARKING SPACE
		4 RAISED PARKING FEE
		5 RENOVATED APARTMENTS AROUND ME
		6 BROUGHT MANY PEOPLE TO LOOK AT MY APARTMENT
		7 OTHER_____(SPECIFY)
		8 DON'T KNOW

18	How many bedrooms does your present condominium unit have?	COL. 27
		1 NONE
		2 ONE
		3 TWO
		4 THREE
		5 FOUR
		6 MORE THAN FOUR
		7 DON'T KNOW

19	How many bedrooms did your former residence have?	COL. 28
		1 NONE
		2 ONE
		3 TWO
		4 THREE
		5 FOUR
		6 MORE THAN FOUR
		7 DON'T KNOW

20	What is the total monthly payment for your condominium, including principal, interest, taxes, condominium fee, and utilities? Is it:	COL. 29 INTERVIEWER: READ	SKIP TO
		1 LESS THAN $300	22
		2 $300-349	22
		3 $350-399	22
		4 $400-449	22
		5 $450-499	22
		6 $500-549	22
		7 $550-599	22
		8 $600 OR MORE	22
		DO NOT READ	
		9 DON'T KNOW/REFUSED	21

21	Can you tell me how much the condominium fee is? Is it:	COL. 30 INTERVIEWER: READ
		1 LESS THAN $100
		2 $100-149
		3 $150-199
		4 $200-249
		5 $250 OR MORE
		DO NOT READ
		6 DON'T KNOW/REFUSED

22	Is the cost of owning your condominium higher, lower, or about the same as the developer said it would be?	COL. 31
		1 HIGHER
		2 LOWER
		3 ABOUT THE SAME
		4 DON'T KNOW

INTERVIEWER: CHECK QUESTION 1. IF RESPONDENT RENTFD HIS/HER PREVIOUS RESIDENCE, ASK QUESTION 23. IF RESPONDENT OWNED HIS/HER PREVIOUS RESIDENCE, SKIP TO QUESTION 24. IF "DON'T KNOW," SKIP TO QUESTION 25.

23	What were your total monthly housing costs when you last rented, including rent and utilities. Were they:	COL. 32	SKIP TO
		1 LESS THAN $200	25
		2 $200-249	25
		3 $250-299	25
		4 $300-349	25
		5 $350-399	25
		6 $400-449	25
		7 $450-499	25
		8 $500 OR MORE	25
		DO NOT READ	
		9 DON'T KNOW/REFUSED	25

24	What were your total monthly housing costs where you owned before, including principal, interest, taxes, condominium fees, and utilities? Were they:	COL. 33 INTERVIEWER: READ	SKIP TO

		COL. 33 INTERVIEWER: READ	SKIP TO
		1 LESS THAN $300	25
		2 $300-349	25
		3 $350-399	25
		4 $400-449	25
		5 $450-499	25
		6 $500-549	25
		7 $550-599	25
		8 $600 OR MORE	25
		DO NOT READ	
		9 DON'T KNOW/REFUSED (see below)	

INTERVIEWER: IF RESPONDENT SAYS "DON'T KNOW/REFUSED," PROBE:
"Can you tell me any of these individual costs, such as
the condominium fee, utilities, taxes, interest, or the
principal?"   WRITE DOWN AND LABEL WHATEVER RESPONDENT
DOES KNOW.

25	What price did you pay for your present condominium unit?	COL. 34 INTERVIEWER: READ
		1 $10,000-19,999
		2 $20,000-29,999
		3 $30,000-39,999
		4 $40,000-49,999
		5 $50,000-59,999
		6 $60,000-69,999
		7 $70,000 AND OVER
		DO NOT READ
		8 DON'T KNOW

26	What percentage of the purchase price did you put toward the down payment?	COL. 35
		1 LESS THAN 10 PERCENT
		2 10 TO 15 PERCENT
		3 16 TO 20 PERCENT
		4 21 TO 25 PERCENT
		5 26 TO 30 PERCENT
		6 MORE THAN 30 PERCENT
		7 DON'T KNOW

27	Who did you get the mortgage from--a bank, a developer (building owner), or somewhere else?	COL. 36
		1 BANK
		2 DEVELOPER
		3 OTHER_____(SPECIFY)
		4 DON'T KNOW/REFUSED

28	Do you have a second mortgage?	COL. 37	SKIP TO
		1 YES	29
		2 NO	30
		3 DON'T KNOW	30

29	What percentage of the pur-chase price does it represent?	COL. 38	
		1	1 TO 9 PERCENT
		2	10 TO 19 PERCENT
		3	20 TO 29 PERCENT
		4	30 TO 39 PERCENT
		5	40 TO 49 PERCENT
		6	50 TO 59 PERCENT
		7	60 PERCENT OR OVER
		8	DON'T KNOW

30	Was the unit vacant when you purchased it?	COL. 39		SKIP TO
		1	YES	34
		2	NO	31
		3	DON'T KNOW	31

31	How did the developer suggest you deal with the occupant?	COL. 40	COL. 41
		1	1
		2	2
		3	3
		4	4
		5	5
		6	6
		7	7
		8	8
		9	9
		0	0
		X	X
		Y	Y

32	How did you deal with the occupant?	COL. 42	COL. 43
		1	1
		2	2
		3	3
		4	4
		5	5
		6	6
		7	7
		8	8
		9	9
		0	0
		X	X
		Y	Y

33	Did the developer offer you a special price or any other inducements if you pur-chased while the unit was occupied?	COL. 44	
		1	YES
		2	NO
		3	DON'T KNOW

34	Did the developer put your unit in good condition?	COL. 45		SKIP TO
		1	YES	36
		2	NO	35
		3	DON'T KNOW	35

35 What did he/she do poorly?	COL. 46	
	1 POOR QUALITY EQUIPMENT (DISHWASHER, DISPOSER, ETC.)	
	2 POOR QUALITY MATERIAL (RUGS, PAPER, ETC.)	
	3 POOR QUALITY WORKMANSHIP	
	4 POOR DESIGN	
	5 OTHER_____(SPECIFY)	
	6 DON'T KNOW	

36 Did the developer put the building in good condition?	COL. 47	SKIP TO
	1 YES	38
	2 NO	37
	3 DON'T KNOW	37

37 What did he/she do poorly?	COL. 48	
	1 POOR WORKMANSHIP	
	2 POOR QUALITY MATERIALS (RUGS, PAPER, ETC.)	
	3 COMMON AREAS POORLY DONE	
	4 UTILITIES BAD (HEAT, HOT WATER, ETC.)	
	5 OTHER_____(SPECIFY)	
	6 DON'T KNOW	

38 Do you plan to sell your condominium unit in the near future?	COL. 49	SKIP TO
	1 YES	39
	2 NO	41
	3 DON'T KNOW	41

39 How soon do you plan to sell your condominium unit?	COL. 50 INTERVIEWER: READ	
	1 WITHIN 1 YEAR	
	2 1 YEAR UP TO 3 YEARS	
	3 3 YEARS UP TO 4 YEARS	
	4 4 YEARS OR MORE	
	DO NOT READ	
	5 DON'T KNOW/REFUSED	

40 What are the one or two most important reasons why you are planning to sell your condominium? (MULTIPLE RESPONSES PERMITTED)	COL. 51	
	1 REALIZE THE INCREASED VALUE	
	2 BUY A LARGER CONDOMINIUM	
	3 BUY A HOUSE	
	4 RENT	
	5 MOVE TO DIFFERENT LOCATION	
	6 OTHER_____(SPECIFY)	
	7 DON'T KNOW	

| 41 | What are the primary advantages you see in owning a condominium? | COL. 52

1 HOUSING COSTS ARE TAX DEDUCTIBLE
2 TAX SHELTER
3 PROTECTION AGAINST RISING HOUSING COSTS
4 GOOD INVESTMENT
5 OWNING IS BETTER THAN RENTING
6 NONE
7 OTHER_____(SPECIFY)
8 DON'T KNOW | |

| 42 | Are some of the units in your building still rented? | COL. 53

1 YES
2 NO
3 DON'T KNOW | SKIP TO

43
44
44 |

| 43 | What kinds of problems has this caused, if any? | COL. 54

1
2
3
4
5
6
7
8
9
0
X
Y | COL. 55

1
2
3
4
5
6
7
8
9
0
X
Y |

| 44 | What is your marital status? Are you: | COL. 56 INTERVIEWER: READ

1 MARRIED
2 SINGLE
3 WIDOWED
4 DIVORCED/SEPARATED
5 OTHER_____(SPECIFY)
DO NOT READ
6 DON'T KNOW/REFUSED | |

| 45 | Do you own this condominium jointly with another adult? | COL. 57

1 YES
2 NO
3 DON'T KNOW | |

| 46 | Including yourself, how many people live in this condominium? | COL. 58

1 ONE
2 TWO
3 THREE
4 FOUR
5 FIVE OR MORE
6 DON'T KNOW/REFUSED | |

47	How many adults live in this condominium?	COL. _59_	
		1	ONE
		2	TWO
		3	THREE
		4	FOUR
		5	FIVE OR MORE
		6	DON'T KNOW/REFUSED

48	How many children do you have living with you?	COL. _60_		SKIP TO
		0	NONE	53
		1	ONE	49
		2	TWO	49
		3	THREE	49
		4	FOUR	49
		5	FIVE	49
		6	SIX	49
		7	SEVEN OR MORE	49
		8	DON'T KNOW/REFUSED	53

49	How many children do you have living with you 5 years of age or under?	COL. _61_	
		0	NONE
		1	ONE
		2	TWO
		3	THREE
		4	FOUR
		5	FIVE
		6	SIX
		7	SEVEN OR MORE
		8	DON'T KNOW/REFUSED

50	How many children do you have living with you between the ages of 6 and 19? (INCLUDES 6-YEAR-OLDS AND 19-YEAR-OLDS)	COL. _62_	
		0	NONE
		1	ONE
		2	TWO
		3	THREE
		4	FOUR
		5	FIVE
		6	SIX
		7	SEVEN OR MORE
		8	DON'T KNOW/REFUSED

51	How many children do you have living with you 20 years of age or older?	COL. _63_	
		0	NONE
		1	ONE
		2	TWO
		3	THREE
		4	FOUR
		5	FIVE
		6	SIX
		7	SEVEN OR MORE
		8	DON'T KNOW/REFUSED

52	Is this a single-parent household?	COL. 64	
		1 YES	
		2 NO	
		3 DON'T KNOW	

53	Are you presently employed?	COL. 65	SKIP TO
		1 YES	54
		2 NO	55
		3 DON'T KNOW	55

54	Into which of the following job categories does your job fall?	COL. 66 INTERVIEWER: READ	SKIP TO
		1 PROFESSIONAL JOB	56
		2 TECHNICAL JOB	56
		3 MANAGERIAL JOB	56
		4 SALES JOB	56
		5 CLERICAL JOB	56
		6 OTHER_____	56
		(SPECIFY)	
		DO NOT READ	
		7 DON'T KNOW/REFUSED	56

55	Are you retired?	COL. 67	
		1 YES	
		2 NO	
		3 DON'T KNOW	

56	Is your spouse (or co-owner) employed?	COL. 68	SKIP TO
		1 YES	57
		2 NO	58
		3 DON'T KNOW	58
		4 NO SPOUSE OR CO-OWNER	59

57	Into which of the following job categories does his/her job fall?	COL. 69 INTERVIEWER: READ	SKIP TO
		1 PROFESSIONAL JOB	59
		2 TECHNICAL JOB	59
		3 MANAGERIAL JOB	59
		4 SALES JOB	59
		5 CLERICAL JOB	59
		6 OTHER_____	59
		(SPECIFY)	
		DO NOT READ	
		7 DON'T KNOW/REFUSED	59

58	Is he/she retired?	COL. 70	
		1 YES	
		2 NO	
		3 DON'T KNOW	

59	Into which of the following categories does your own age fall?	COL. 71 INTERVIEWER: READ

COL. 71 INTERVIEWER: READ

1 UNDER 21
2 21-30
3 31-40
4 41-50
5 51-60
6 61-70
7 71 AND OVER
DO NOT READ
8 DON'T KNOW/REFUSED

60 Finally, into which of the following categories did your total family income fall in 1978?

COL. 72 INTERVIEWER: READ

1 UNDER $10,000
2 $10,000-19,999
3 $20,000-29,999
4 $30,000-39,999
5 $40,000-49,999
6 $50,000 AND OVER
DO NOT READ
7 DON'T KNOW

61 What is the primary source of income for this household?

COL. 73

1 SALARY AND WAGES
2 INTEREST & DIVIDENDS
3 SELF-EMPLOYED
4 SOCIAL SECURITY/PENSION
5 PUBLIC ASSISTANCE
6 TRUST FUND
7 OTHER
8 DON'T KNOW/REFUSED

And your address is . . .

ADDRESS_____ CITY_____ ZIP_____

TELEPHONE NUMBER_____ DATE_____

Thank respondent for his/her cooperation.

Interviewer's signature_____

DO NOT COMPLETE

NUMBER OF UNITS IN THE BUILDING

COL. 74   COL. 75

1 | 7   1 | 7
2 | 8   2 | 8
3 | 9   3 | 9
4 | 0   4 | 0
5 | X   5 | X
6 | Y   6 | Y

Project #4361

Interviewing begins:

DISPLACED FORMER TENANTS

Hello, I'm calling from Becker
Research Corporation of Boston.
We are doing a survey for the
town selectmen in Brookline
in order to get people's reactions and concerns about
the conversion of apartments
to condominiums. The survey
is among people who were
forced to move because their
buildings were converted into
condominiums. I would like to
speak with the head of the
household.

INTERVIEWER: DO NOT COMPLETE

I.D.#

__COL. 1 1 2 3 4 5 6 7 8 9 0
__COL. 2 1 2 3 4 5 6 7 8 9 0
__COL. 3 1 2 3 4 5 6 7 8 9 0
__COL. 4 1 2 3 4 5 6 7 8 9 0
__COL. 5 1 2 3 4 5 6 7 8 9 0

INTERVIEWER: COMPLETE

COL. 8   1 MALE   2 FEMALE

---

1 As you were forced to move, in what ways did the move most affect your life?

COL. 9

1
2
3
4
5
6
7
8
9
0
X
Y

COL. 10

1
2
3
4
5
6
7
8
9
0
X
Y

---

2 To begin with, as compared to the apartment you were evicted from, would you say the place you live in now is better, worse, or the same as your previous apartment?

COL. 11

1 BETTER
2 SAME
3 WORSE
4 DON'T KNOW

---

3   What are the most important differences between your present
    residence and your previous apartment?

    COL. 12

    1   RENT (COST OF OWNERSHIP) IS HIGHER HERE
    2   THIS PLACE NOT AS LARGE
    3   THIS APARTMENT NOT AS NICE
    4   THIS BUILDING NOT AS NICE
    5   THIS NEIGHBORHOOD NOT AS GOOD
    6   SCHOOLS HERE NOT AS GOOD
    7   TOWN SERVICES HERE NOT AS GOOD
    8   OTHER_____(SPECIFY)
    9   DON'T KNOW

    COL. 13

    1   RENT (COST OF OWNERSHIP) LOWER HERE
    2   THIS PLACE LARGER
    3   THIS APARTMENT NICER
    4   THIS BUILDING NICER
    5   THIS NEIGHBORHOOD BETTER
    6   SCHOOLS HERE ARE BETTER
    7   TOWN SERVICES ARE BETTER
    8   OTHER_____SPECIFY)
    9   DON'T KNOW

4   As compared to your previous apartment, is your present
    residence more convenient to or less convenient to:

INTERVIEWER: READ	LESS	MORE	COL.
JOB	1	2	14
SHOPPING	1	2	15
FRIENDS/FAMILY	1	2	16
PUBLIC TRANSPORTATION	1	2	17
DO NOT READ			
OTHER_____(SPECIFY)	1	2	18

5   When you were living in   COL. 19
    your previous (converted)
    apartment, how did you   1   NOTICE BY LANDLORD (LETTER,
    first hear about plans   OFFICIAL NOTICE, ETC.)
    to convert the building   2   RUMOR (FROM NEIGHBORS, ETC.)
    from rentals to condo-   3   OTHER_____(SPECIFY)
    miniums?   4   DON'T KNOW

6   What were your reactions   COL. 20   COL. 21
    when you first heard about
    these plans?   1 | 7   1 | 7
                                 2 | 8   2 | 8
                                 3 | 9   3 | 9
                                 4 | 0   4 | 0
                                 5 | X   5 | X
                                 6 | Y   6 | Y

7	Had the landlord sold your apartment as a condominium to another owner before you moved?	COL. 22 1 YES 2 NO 3 DON'T KNOW	
8	When you were given a date by which you had to be out of your apartment, how much time were you given to vacate?	COL. 23 1 LESS THAN 1 WEEK 2 1 WEEK TO 1 MONTH 3 MORE THAN 1 MONTH TO 3 MONTHS 4 MORE THAN 3 MONTHS TO 6 MONTHS 5 MORE THAN 6 MONTHS 6 DON'T KNOW	
9	How long did you have to look to find the place you moved to?	COL. 24 1 LESS THAN 1 WEEK 2 1 WEEK TO 1 MONTH 3 MORE THAN 1 MONTH TO 3 MONTHS 4 MORE THAN 3 MONTHS TO 6 MONTHS 5 MORE THAN 6 MONTHS 6 DON'T KNOW	

10	How difficult was it to find what you wanted? Was it very difficult, fairly difficult, or not at all difficult?	COL. 25	SKIP TO
		1 VERY DIFFICULT	11
		2 FAIRLY DIFFICULT	11
		3 NOT VERY DIFFICULT	12
		4 NOT AT ALL DIFFI- CULT	12
		5 DON'T KNOW	12

11	Why was it difficult?	COL. 26
		
		1 RENTS TOO HIGH
		2 COULDN'T FIND THE SIZE APART-
		    MENT I WANTED
		3 COULDN'T FIND THE QUALITY
		    APARTMENT I WANTED
		4 COULDN'T FIND A GOOD LOCATION
		5 OTHER_____(SPECIFY)
		6 DON'T KNOW	

12	Did your former landlord offer to help you find replacement housing?	COL. 27	SKIP TO
		1 YES	13
		2 NO	14
		3 DON'T KNOW	14

13 How did he/she help you?	COL. 28	COL. 29
	1	1
	2	2
	3	3
	4	4
	5	5
	6	6
	7	7
	8	8
	9	9
	0	0
	X	X
	Y	Y

14 Did your former landlord cause you any trouble after giving you notice to vacate?	COL. 30	SKIP TO
	1 YES	15
	2 NO	16
	3 DON'T KNOW	16

15 What did he/she do? COL. 31

1   TRIED TO RAISE RENT
2   SENT THREATENING LETTER
3   TOOK/TRIED TO TAKE PARKING SPACE
4   RAISED PARKING FEES
5   RENOVATED APARTMENTS AROUND ME
6   BROUGHT MANY PEOPLE TO LOOK AT MY APARTMENT
7   TRIED TO PRESSURE ME INTO BUYING
8   OTHER_____(SPECIFY)
9   DON'T KNOW

16 During the twelve months preceding conversion of your apartment to a condominium unit, did your former landlord petition the rent control board for an increase in the rent of your apartment?	COL. 32	SKIP TO
	1 YES	17
	2 NO	19
	3 DON'T KNOW	19

17 What was the amount of the increase your landlord was seeking? COL. 33

1   $10-50 PER MONTH
2   $51-100 PER MONTH
3   $101-150 PER MONTH
4   MORE THAN $150 PER MONTH
5   DON'T KNOW

18 Was it granted? COL. 34

1   YES
2   NO
3   DON'T KNOW

19	After the conversion of your apartment building to condominiums, did your former landlord petition the rent control board for an increase in the rent of your apartment?	COL. 35 1 YES 2 NO 3 DON'T KNOW	SKIP TO 20 22 22
20	What was the amount of the increase your landlord was seeking?	COL. 36 1 $10-$50 PER MONTH 2 $51-100 PER MONTH 3 $101-150 PER MONTH 4 MORE THAN $150 PER MONTH 5 DON'T KNOW	
21	Was it granted?	COL. 37 1 YES 2 NO 3 DON'T KNOW	
22	Did your former landlord make any physical improvements in your apartment that you did not request during the twelve months prior to the time it was converted into a condominium?	COL. 38 1 YES 2 NO 3 DON'T KNOW	
23	Did your former landlord cut back on any service during the twelve months prior to the time your apartment was converted to a condominium unit?	COL. 39 1 YES 2 NO 3 DON'T KNOW	
24	When your former apartment was converted to a condominium unit, what was the offering price (to you)?	COL. 40 1 UNDER $20,000 2 $20,000-29,999 3 $30,000-39,999 4 $40,000-49,999 5 $50,000-59,999 6 $60,000-69,999 7 $70,000-79,999 8 $80,000 AND OVER 9 DON'T KNOW	
25	Did the landlord tell you this was below what he was offering to non-tenants?	COL. 41 1 YES 2 NO 3 DON'T KNOW	

26	Had you considered moving out of your former apartment before you first heard about plans to convert the building from rental to condominium?	COL. 42 1 YES 2 NO 3 DON'T KNOW	SKIP TO 27 28 28
27	Why had you considered moving?	COL. 43 1 THE APARTMENT HAD PROBLEMS 2 I DIDN'T WANT TO LIVE IN THAT NEIGHBORHOOD ANY LONGER 3 THE LANDLORD GAVE BAD SERVICE 4 RENTS GOT TOO HIGH 5 OTHER____ (SPECIFY) 6 DON'T KNOW	
28	When your former apartment was actually converted to a condominium unit, why did you move? (MULTIPLE RESPONSES PERMITTED)	COL. 44 1 I WAS TOO OLD TO BUY A CONDO-MINIUM 2 THE OFFERING PRICE WAS TOO EXPENSIVE FOR ME 3 I DIDN'T WANT TO OWN A CONDO-MINIUM 4 THE BUILDING HAD PROBLEMS 5 I DIDN'T WANT TO CONTINUE LIVING IN THE NEIGHBORHOOD 6 I THOUGHT A CONDOMINIUM WAS A BAD INVESTMENT 7 I DIDN'T HAVE ENOUGH INFORMA-TION 8 I DIDN'T HAVE ENOUGH TIME TO CONSIDER THE PURCHASE 9 OTHER_____ (SPECIFY) 0 DON'T KNOW	
29	What was the address of your previous apartment that was converted to a condominium? _____ _____	COL. 45 1 2 3 4 5 6 7 8 9 0 X Y	COL. 46 1 2 3 4 5 6 7 8 9 0 X Y

30	When did you move from it?	COL. 47		COL. 48	
		1	JAN	1	1970
		2	FEB	2	1971
		3	MARCH	3	1972
		4	APRIL	4	1973
		5	MAY	5	1974
		6	JUNE	6	1975
		7	JULY	7	1976
		8	AUGUST	8	1977
		9	SEPT	9	1978
		0	OCT	0	1979
		X	NOV	X	
		Y	DEC	Y	

31	How long had you and the other members of your household lived in the converted apartment?	COL. 49	
		1	LESS THAN 1 MONTH
		2	1-3 MONTHS
		3	4-6 MONTHS
		4	7-12 MONTHS
		5	13-18 MONTHS
		6	19-24 MONTHS
		7	25-36 MONTHS
		8	3-5 YEARS
		9	MORE THAN 5 YEARS
		0	DON'T KNOW

32	What was your marital status when you were forced to move?	COL. 50 INTERVIEWER: READ		SKIP TO
		1	MARRIED	34
		2	SINGLE	33
		3	WIDOWED	33
		4	DIVORCED/SEPARATED	33
		5	OTHER _____ (SPECIFY)	33
			DO NOT READ	
		6	DON'T KNOW/REFUSED	33

33	Did you share your previous apartment with another adult?	COL. 51	
		1	YES
		2	NO
		3	DON'T KNOW

34	Including yourself, how many people were living in your previous apartment?	COL. 52	
		1	ONE
		2	TWO
		3	THREE
		4	FOUR
		5	FIVE OR MORE
		6	DON'T KNOW

35	How many adults were living in your previous apartment when you moved?	COL. 53

1 ONE
2 TWO
3 THREE
4 FOUR
5 FIVE OR MORE
6 DON'T KNOW

36	How many children did you have living with you when you moved?	COL. 54	SKIP TO

0 NONE   41
1 ONE
2 TWO
3 THREE
4 FOUR
5 FIVE
6 SIX
7 SEVEN OR MORE
8 DON'T KNOW/REFUSED 41

37	How many children did you have living with you when you moved who were five years of age or under?	COL. 55

0 NONE
1 ONE
2 TWO
3 THREE
4 FOUR
5 FIVE
6 SIX
7 SEVEN OR MORE
8 DON'T KNOW/REFUSED

38	How many children did you have living with you when you moved who were between the ages of 6 and 19? (INCLUDES 6-YEAR-OLDS AND 19-YEAR-OLDS)	COL. 56

0 NONE
1 ONE
2 TWO
3 THREE
4 FOUR
5 FIVE
6 SIX
7 SEVEN OR MORE
8 DON'T KNOW/REFUSED

39	How many children did you have living with you when you moved who were 20 years of age or older?	COL. 57

0 NONE
1 ONE
2 TWO
3 THREE
4 FOUR
5 FIVE
6 SIX
7 SEVEN OR MORE
8 DON'T KNOW/REFUSED

40	Was your household a single-parent household when you moved?	COL. 58	
		1 YES	
		2 NO	
		3 DON'T KNOW	

41	Were you employed at the time when you moved?	COL. 59	SKIP TO
		1 YES	42
		2 NO	43
		3 DON'T KNOW	43

42	When you moved, into which of the following job categories did your job fall?	COL. 60 INTERVIEWER: READ	SKIP TO
		1 PROFESSIONAL JOB	44
		2 TECHNICAL JOB	44
		3 MANAGERIAL JOB	44
		4 SALES JOB	44
		5 CLERICAL JOB	44
		6 OTHER_____ (SPECIFY)	44
		DO NOT READ	
		7 DON'T KNOW/REFUSED	44

43	Were you retired at that time?	COL. 61	
		1 YES	
		2 NO	
		3 DON'T KNOW	

44	Was your spouse (or other principal member of household) employed at the time when you moved?	COL. 62	SKIP TO
		1 YES	45
		2 NO	46
		3 DON'T KNOW	46
		4 NO SPOUSE	46

45	When you moved, into which of the following job categories did his/her job fall?	COL. 63 INTERVIEWER: READ	SKIP TO
		1 PROFESSIONAL JOB	47
		2 TECHNICAL JOB	47
		3 MANAGERIAL JOB	47
		4 SALES JOB	47
		5 CLERICAL JOB	47
		6 OTHER_____ (SPECIFY)	47
		DO NOT READ	
		7 DON'T KNOW/REFUSED	47

46	Was he/she retired at that time?	COL. 64	
		1 YES	
		2 NO	
		3 DON'T KNOW	

47	What was the total monthly rent (with utilities) of your previous apartment?	COL. 65

1   LESS THAN $200
2   $200-299
3   $300-399
4   $400-500
5   OVER $500
6   DON'T KNOW/REFUSED

48	Do you presently rent an apartment or house or do you own a house or condominium (apartment)?	COL. 66	SKIP TO

1   RENT APARTMENT   49
2   RENT HOUSE   49
3   OWN HOUSE   50
4   OWN CONDOMINIUM   50
5   OTHER_____   52
       (SPECIFY)
6   DON'T KNOW   52

49	What is the total monthly rent (with utilities) for your present apartment or house?	COL. 67	SKIP TO

1   LESS THAN $200   52
2   $200-299   52
3   $300-399   52
4   $400-500   52
5   OVER $500   52
6   DON'T KNOW/REFUSED   52

50	What is the total monthly carrying cost of your present house/condominium (principal, interest, taxes, utilities, fees)?	COL. 68

1   LESS THAN $200
2   $200-299
3   $300-399
4   $400-499
5   $500-600
6   OVER $600
7   DON'T KNOW/REFUSED

51	What price did you pay for your present dwelling?	COL. 69

1   UNDER $29,999
2   $30,000-39,999
3   $40,000-49,999
4   $50,000-59,999
5   $60,000-69,999
6   $70,000 OR MORE
7   DON'T KNOW/REFUSED

52	How many bedrooms does your present apartment (house, condominium) have?	COL. 70

0   NONE
1   ONE
2   TWO
3   THREE
4   FOUR
5   MORE THAN FOUR
6   DON'T KNOW/REFUSED

53	How many bedrooms did your previous apartment have?	COL. 71	
		0	NONE
		1	ONE
		2	TWO
		3	THREE
		4	FOUR
		5	MORE THAN FOUR
		6	DON'T KNOW/REFUSED

54	Into which of the following categories does your own age fall?	COL. 72 INTERVIEWER: READ	
		1	UNDER 21
		2	21-30
		3	31-40
		4	41-50
		5	51-60
		6	61-70
		7	71 AND OVER
			DO NOT READ
		8	DON'T KNOW/REFUSED

55	Finally, into which of the following categories did your total family income fall in 1978?	COL. 73 INTERVIEWER: READ	
		1	UNDER $10,000
		2	$10,000-19,999
		3	$20,000-29,999
		4	$30,000-39,999
		5	$40,000-49,999
		6	$50,000 AND OVER
			DO NOT READ
		7	DON'T KNOW/REFUSED

56	What is the primary source of income for this household?	COL. 74	
		1	SALARY & WAGES
		2	INTEREST & DIVIDENDS
		3	SELF-EMPLOYED
		4	SOCIAL SECURITY/PENSION
		5	PUBLIC ASSISTANCE
		6	TRUST FUND
		7	OTHER
		8	DON'T KNOW/REFUSED

And your address is . . .

ADDRESS_____ CITY_____ ZIP_____

TELEPHONE NUMBER_____ DATE_____

Thank respondent for his/her cooperation.

Interviewer's signature_____

Appendix B

SURVEY METHODOLOGY

All survey interviewing was carried out by Becker Research Corporation under the direction of Harbridge House, Inc. The sample for each of the four interview groups was constructed in a somewhat different way, as described below.

Renters in Controlled Units

In selecting interviewees, a reverse telephone directory, a directory of telephone numbers listed alphabetically by street and by house number on each street, was the basic tool. The directory used was based on the Boston telephone book issued October 1978. A list of all rent controlled buildings, arranged by address, was obtained from Brookline's Information Services Department. A sample of these addresses was selected and marked on each page of the reverse directory. The individuals to be called were every tenth name listed in the designated buildings. Interviewers were instructed to go to the next listed name if the person selected was not home, refused to be interviewed, or did not complete the interview.

The interviewers were instructed to ask for the head of the household and also to try to maintain a balance between males and females. Interviewers were subject to continual monitoring while conducting the interviews, and each filled-in form was reviewed for completeness and legibility before acceptance. Omissions or ambiguous recordings of data were remedied by call-backs. Interviewing was done primarily in the evenings and on weekends.

Condominium Owners

Based on a list of converted buildings supplied by the Town Assessor's Office, condominiums were noted in the reverse telephone directory. An initial effort was made to follow a calling pattern similar to that used for the renters. When it became impossible to meet the quota of calls (300) by this means, interviewers were instructed to call all names listed for each converted building. Because so many condominium owners had moved in since the telephone directory had been published, this procedure resulted in only about 225 interviews. An additional list of over one hundred names was then obtained from the mailboxes of more recently converted buildings, and telephone numbers for these persons were obtained from the telephone company. (This procedure also produced interviews with 84 renters in converted buildings.) The monitoring and verification procedures used for renters were followed for condominium owners.

Displaced Tenants

A list of names and addresses of 75 former tenants of converted buildings was obtained from various tenant groups and from individuals by a member of the Condominium Study Committee. Becker Research staff attempted to obtain phone numbers for persons whose numbers were not listed (persons comprising most of the list), but incomplete or incorrect names and addresses made this impossible in many cases. All persons who could be reached were reached, no matter where they lived.

Interview Attempts and Completions

A "score card" of calls dialed and completed and interviews attempted and completed for each group of interviewees is shown in Exhibit B.1.

Exhibit B.1 Telephone Interview Tally

	Rent Control Tenants	Condominium Owners/ Renters in Condominium Buildings	Displaced Tenants
Dialings	4,618	2,525	124
Completions	2,001	1,061	47
Refusals	532	273	14
Terminations	103	54	1
Ineligibles	565	358	10°
Interviews	801	377	22

° Claimed not to have been displaced.

Validity Tests

Are the two principal survey samples—of current renters and of condominium owners—representative of the total population of these groups in Brookline? Three tests are available to answer this question, tests that deal with unit rather than personal characteristics. The analysis of the rent levels in all rent controlled units in Brookline described in Appendix C provides a weighted average rent for all such units. Because rents for units larger than three bedrooms were not specified in this analysis, some additional estimating was required. The weighted rent of this universe, adjusted for larger units, is $310–315 per month. The weighted rent of our sample was $345. Given the necessity of weighting rents by the mid-points of a range (for example, $350–400 would be weighted as $375), this match appears to be fairly good—about a 10 percent variance.

A similar test may be applied for condominium prices. The average price for all units sold in Brookline from 1976 through 1979 was $39,664. The weighted average of our sample was about $37,263—a difference of 6 percent. Since the questionnaire asked only about price range, not actual price, this also appears to be a good match.

Exhibit C.2 in Appendix C shows the number of rent controlled units of each size (efficiencies; one-, two-, and three-bedroom apartments; apartments with more than three bedrooms) in the Brookline Rent Control Boari's files as of July 1, 1979. A comparison between their size distribution and that in our sample of 891 units is shown in

Exhibit B.2 Size Distribution of Rental Units by Number of Bedrooms: Study Sample vs. Rent Control Board Files

	Rent Board Files		*Study Sample*		
No. of Bedrooms	*No. of Units*	*% of Total*	*No. of Units*	*% of Total*	*% Difference*
Efficiency	441	4.8	38	4.5	− .3
1	3244	35.5	296	33.2	−2.3
2	3490	38.2	333	37.7	− .5
3	1319	14.5	145	16.3	+1.8
More than 3	633	6.9	79	8.9	+2.0
TOTAL	9127°	100	891	100	

° Excludes 63 units for which number of bedrooms was not specified.

Exhibit B.2. The distribution is quite similar, with no more than 2.3 percentage points difference within any category.

While these tests are not definitive, they show that there are no major abnormalities in our samples as compared with all apartments or condominiums in Brookline.

Appendix C

RENTAL HOUSING STOCK

At the request of Harbridge House, Inc., Brookline's Information Services Department prepared a special tabulation analyzing the 1979 rent controlled stock by size and rent. The data were analyzed, aggregated, and displayed in a 24-cell matrix, shown in Exhibit C.1. Each cell shows a designated rent range for a specific size of apartment. The completed matrix is shown in Exhibit C.2 for rent controlled units in unconverted buildings and in Exhibit C.3 for rent controlled units in converted buildings. The rent ranges in each cell were established by Harbridge House in consultation with Rent Control Board staff members.

The data for the tabulation were compiled from computer tapes containing file data current as of July 1, 1979. The data for units in converted buildings, however, are in fact current as of some earlier,

Exhibit C.1   Categorization of Rents in Rent Controlled Apartments by Size of Unit

| Rent Category | Efficiency | No. of Bedrooms | | |
		1	2	3
1	<$100	<150	<200	<200
2	100–149	150–199	200–249	200–249
3	150–199	200–249	250–299	250–299
4	200–249	250–299	300–349	300–349
5	250–299	300–399	350–449	350–499
6	300+	400+	450+	500+

Exhibit C.2   Actual Rents of Rent Controlled Apartments in Unconverted Buildings in Relation to Unit Size

| Rent Category | No. of Bedrooms | | | | Total Units |
	Efficiency	1	2	3	
1	1	156	197	145	499
2	17	369	429	139	954
3	98	954	833	203	2088
4	142	1115	1115	254	2626
5	95	508	657	495	1755
6	88	142	259	83	572
TOTAL	441	3244	3490	1319	8494

No. of Units (all sizes) = 9190
Building Weight = 3.69
No. of Units > 3 Bedrooms = 633

Distribution of Weighted Building Rent Averages

Weighted Building Rent Category	No. of Buildings
1.00–1.5	114
1.51–2.5	133
2.51–3.5	222
3.51–4.5	262
4.51–5.5	134
5.51–6.0	15
Missing (empty cells)	91
TOTAL	971

unspecifiable date. This circumstance is due to the lead times between the filing of a master deed for conversion, the recording of a building as a condominium in the Assessor's Office records, and the subsequent change in its status in the Rent Control Board files. The total time involved may be as much as thirteen months.

Only the summary sheets for the two tabulations are presented here. Each building has a separate page in the computer printout, with the matrix appropriately filled in. The summary shows the number of units of each size and rent range in all rent controlled buildings. Thus, reading across the bottom line of the summary sheet will give the total number of efficiencies and one-, two-, and three-bedroom units. Reading down the right side will show the total of all units of all four sizes in each of the six rent categories. The unit rent for different size units, of course, varies within each of the categories.

Exhibit C.3 Actual Rents of Rent Controlled Units in Converted Buildings in Relation to Unit Size

	No. of Bedrooms				Total
Rent Category	*Efficiency*	*1*	*2*	*3*	*Units*
1	0	7	19	8	34
2	1	10	50	22	83
3	0	18	49	51	118
4	7	40	31	12	90
5	1	136	35	24	196
6	0	33	79	7	119
TOTAL	9	244	263	124	640

No. of Units (all sizes) = 669
Building Weight = 4.07
No. of Units > 3 Bedrooms = 29

Distribution of Weighted Building Rent Averages

Weighted Building Rent Category	*No. of Buildings*
1.001.5	5
1.512.5	1
2.513.5	8
3.514.5	8
4.515.5	6
5.516.0	2
Missing (empty cells)	0
TOTAL	30

A weighted average rent for each building was calculated and is expressed in decimal form. Thus "2.5" means that the weighted average of rents in that building is exactly halfway between rent categories 2 and 3. The distribution of all buildings by weighted rent is 3.69. The total number of all buildings is 971.

A similar summary for all units in converted buildings is shown in Exhibit C.3.

Appendix D

METHODOLOGICAL NOTES

Condominium Carrying Costs

Tables 6.33 and 6.34 present calculations that translate pre-conversion rents into post-conversion carrying charges after taxes. The methodology to accomplish these calculations is described below.

Median income and gross monthly rent estimates were calculated from the results of the survey of 891 renters. These income and rent figures were then used to calculate rent/income ratios for each income range. The projected condominium offering prices for units at each rent were established by multiplying the gross monthly rent figures by the sales price/rent ratio as described in Chapter 3.

Monthly carrying costs for a condominium unit were calculated through a multi-step process. First, the mortgage principal was calculated by assuming a 25-year amortization period, a 75 percent mortgage, a 25 percent down payment, and no second mortgage. The down payment percentage is representative of that reported by condominium owners in the sample. The amortization and interest rates are those typically reported in interviews with bankers. Next, an amortization schedule for the mortgage was determined. (See Exhibit D.1 for the formula by which this schedule was determined.) This schedule produces the yearly payments for principal and interest for any given mortgage principal. To this amount were added property taxes, based on the formula shown on page 195 for estimating property taxes from pre-conversion rents, and condominium

Exhibit D.1   Formulas for Determination of Amortization Schedule

Amortization Formula

$$PV = \frac{PMT}{i}\left[1-(1+i)^{-n}\right] + BAL\,(1+i)^{-n}$$

Accumulated Interest Formula

$$BAL_k = \frac{1}{(-1+i)^{-k}}\left[PMT\,\frac{(1+i)^{-k}-1}{i}+PV\right]$$

$$INT_{j-k} = BAL_k - BAL_{j-1} + (K-J+1)\,PMT$$

Where:

PV = present value
PMT = payment
i = periodic interest rate
BAL = balance
INT = interest (in \$)
k^{th} payment to principal = $BAL_{k+1} - BAL_j$
k^{th} payment to interest = $PMT - (BAL_{k+1} - BAL_j)$
Total payment to interest = $(k) \times (PMT) - (PV - BAL_k)$

Source: S. W. Hamilton and D. D. Ulinder, *Valuation Tables for Real Estate Analysis*, 4th ed. (Vancouver, B.C.: University of British Columbia, 1978).

association fees. The fees, which were based on those reported by the sample of owners, averaged \$1440 per year. These calculations produced the gross unit carrying cost, which includes principal, interest, property tax, and association fee.

To estimate the net carrying cost, tax deductions were estimated. Mortgage interest and property taxes are generally deductible. The marginal tax rate for single persons and for married couples without dependents were separately calculated for each income tax bracket, and the resulting tax savings were then subtracted from the gross carrying cost to produce the net carrying costs, shown in the tables.

Post-Conversion Tax Assessments

As discussed in Chapter 3, post-conversion assessments have a clear though indirect relationship to pre-conversion monthly rents. To estimate post-conversion tax assessments, it was necessary to establish a statistically reliable model of this relationship. This relationship was estimated by using a form of linear regression model, a mathematical way of describing the statistical relationship that exists between two quantities. Data used to derive the formula were taken from the sample of 21 buildings. The formula derived is

$$\begin{matrix} \text{Condominium assessments} \\ \text{for all units in one building} \end{matrix} = \sum_{i=1}^{N} (\text{monthly rent}_i) \times 52 - \$4,086.$$

This formula asserts that the best estimate for the post-conversion assessment of the units in a particular building in this sample can be determined by multiplying the pre-conversion rent for each unit by 52, summing the products of these multiplications, and then subtracting $4,086 from the sum of the products. The arithmetic calculations described by the formula are simply those that statistically have the best chance of predicting post-conversion tax assessments based on preconversion rents.

To apply this formula to the universes of buildings in Hypotheses 1 and 2 requires holding constant two key variables that describe the original sample of 21 buildings. These variables are the proportions of high-, medium-, and low-priced units in the total of all units and the sales price/rent ratios of each of these price classes. Because this was done for both of these hypotheses, the results—that is, the estimated post-conversion assessments—will have the same statistical reliability as the total assessments for the original sample of 21 provided that the town's assessing practices for condominiums do not change.

INDEX

Acquisition
  as percentage of sale price, 37
  sample costs, 45, 46, 47
Adversary relationship, between developers and tenants, 57, 60, 65, 71, 75, 144
Advertising, 32 (*see also* Marketing)
Age (*see also* Elderly)
  of condominium owners, 76–89
  of displaced tenants, 108–109
  of tenants, 89–109
Amenities, as ownership motivation, 16, 17
Amortization schedule, formulas for, 194
Apartment building(s)
  conversion process outlined, 23–24
  converted vs. non-converted, 53–55
  and 100 percent valuation, 133
  owners vs. tenants, 144–145
  projected rate of conversion, 122–128
  rehabilitation of, 28–30, 48
  and rental housing stock survey, 189–191
  selection for conversion, 25–26, 33, 48
  valuation methods for, 118–121
Assessment, 117
  and conversion policy issues, 146
  formulas for, 194
  and 100 percent valuation, 132
  tax implications conversion models, 130–132

Back Bay, Boston (*see also* Boston)
  and condominium prices, 124

  condominiums in, 14
  rehabilitation in, 35
Banks (*see also* Loans; Mortgages)
  and conversion financing, 8, 26–28
  and future conversion rate, 123
  and preference for single-family home mortgages, 125
  and presales as loan factor, 29, 58–59
  and unit purchaser's mortgage, 34–35
Banks, commercial
  and conversion financing, 27
  risks and returns in conversion, 38–39
Banks, savings
  and conversion financing, 27
  risks and returns in conversion, 40–41
Bargaining relationship, between tenants and developers, 59–60
Boston (*see also* Back Bay; Cambridge; Newton)
  conversion in, 3, 4
  conversion rate of, 5
  CPI housing component for, 19–20
  housing market in, 2
Brookline
  average price of condominiums in, 20, 21
  budgetary implications of conversion, 134–139
  condominium owners in, 76–89
  displaced tenants in, 107–109
  eviction ban in, 62, 71, 126–128
  extent of conversion in, 49–55
  Housing Study Committee, 137

DATE DUE

DEMCO 38-297